Preschoolers at Play

Choosing the Right Stuff for Learning & Development

Lisa Mufson Bresson & Megan King

National Association for the Education of Young Children
Washington, DC

National Association for the
Education of Young Children

1401 H Street NW, Suite 600
Washington, DC 20005
202-232-8777 • 800-424-2460
NAEYC.org

NAEYC Books

**Senior Director, Publishing
& Content Development**
Susan Friedman

Director, Books
Dana Battaglia

Senior Editor
Holly Bohart

Editor II
Rossella Procopio

Senior Creative Design Manager
Charity Coleman

Senior Creative Design Specialist
Gillian Frank

**Publishing Business
Operations Manager**
Francine Markowitz

Through its publications program, the National Association for the Education of Young Children (NAEYC) provides a forum for discussion of major issues and ideas in the early childhood field, with the hope of provoking thought and promoting professional growth. The views expressed or implied in this book are not necessarily those of the Association.

Permissions

NAEYC accepts requests for limited use of our copyrighted material. For permission to reprint, adapt, translate, or otherwise reuse and repurpose content from this publication, review our guidelines at **NAEYC.org/resources/permissions.**

Photo Credits

Copyright © Getty Images: cover, iv, 2, 4, 6, 7, 8, 10, 13, 18, 24, 30, 32, 36, 41, 43, 54, 60, 61, 64, 69, 72, 77, 82, 84, 90, 96, 106, 111, 112, 115, and 116

Courtesy of the authors: 16 (both), 22, 35, 38, 44, 47, 48, 50, 53, 55, 71, 78, 86, 92, 99, 101, 102, 105, 110, and 120

Library of Congress Control Number: 2021933109

ISBN: 978-1-938113-76-5

Item: 1150

Contents

Introduction

An Invitation

Consider this book an invitation to think deeply about the play materials you include in your preschool learning setting and how they—and you—can enhance children's learning and development.

Think about someone important to you: a spouse, a child, a sibling, a parent, or a dear friend. What motivates that person to be creative and thoughtful? Have you ever observed that person so deeply engrossed in an activity (reading a book, embroidering a design, preparing a meal) that they hardly know you're there? As we grow, our play transforms into the hobbies and interests that shape and define us. We continue to learn about and better understand the world through the materials we collect and create.

As you make your way through this book, examine yourself as an adult learner. What are *your* favorite things to wonder about? What materials do *you* like to play with? Do you enjoy tinkering in the garage or the garden? Gathering with friends, making others laugh, and delighting in shared storytelling? How about journaling, doodling, dancing, sewing, or playing an instrument? Reflect on your experiences and motivators, see yourself as a joy seeker, and reimagine what play means to you. Through this process of self-reflection, you will nurture a mindset that will help you to think more intentionally and creatively about the materials you include in your early learning setting and how they contribute to an environment that is accessible, inclusive, equitable, and welcoming of all children.

In many ways, our process while writing this book reflects how we hope preschool educators will embrace and use it in their practice. We made a concerted effort to recognize the changing early childhood landscape and incorporate technology. Similar to how teachers consider and respect children's vast and diverse familial, cultural, and developmental journeys, we sought to honor the diversity of our perspectives, celebrated collective ideas, and integrated our individual styles and interests.

Together, we reflected on our deep connection to play and learning. We recalled stories of our own experiences as teachers, some of which we share throughout the book, and spent time in early learning settings in a wide variety of programs and communities. And, of course, the most important part of the process: we talked. We asked each other questions, wondered out loud, and watched ideas blossom, just as we hope you will share your thoughts, ideas, and inspirations with your colleagues and others who are passionate about the field of early childhood education.

Sections of this book were crafted while engaging with some of *our* favorite playful materials and activities: a favorite coffee mug, a pair of fluffy pajamas, a beanbag chair, sets of colorful markers and highlighters, and brisk walks with our dogs in the crisp night air. Herein lies the heart of this book and the process of its becoming: considering the importance of supporting creativity and learning with the right materials and conversations.

We hope you will celebrate the relationships that grow out of deeper understandings of and new perspectives on the play materials you curate and the learning environment you shape for young children.

About this Book

This book overviews familiar, time-honored play materials as well as some newer ones. In addition to highlighting specific, developmentally appropriate materials to include in your early learning setting, it also provides unique perspectives on ways to use these play materials and encourages you to look at them in a new light. The book is designed to be a resource for preschool professionals who work directly with children or who provide practice-based coaching to those who do.

Part One: Essential Questions addresses the who, why, how, and what of curating the "right stuff" for preschool learning settings. This part provides insight into the development of 3- to 5-year-old children, how to choose play materials and organize them in the learning environment, and considerations about the families and communities you serve. While there are many threads woven throughout this book, we continue to highlight one of the most crucial approaches to teaching: *Always consider the individual needs, interests, and prior experiences of each child and all the gifts they come bearing.*

The other three parts of the book each focus on a specific domain of learning and development:

> **Part Two: Cognitive Learning and Development**

> **Part Three: Social and Emotional Learning and Development**

> **Part Four: Physical Learning and Development**

These parts contain four to five chapters that explore play materials and discuss how they support different aspects related to that domain. Each chapter begins with an overview of suggested play materials and why they are important to incorporate in your early learning setting. These include a range of store-bought, found, and natural play materials.

Select materials are highlighted in a more in-depth way. Alongside the descriptions of play materials are ideas for creative and appropriate ways to scaffold and extend children's thinking. Research on play and the way children engage in play is incorporated throughout.

We believe the most effective use of technology in preschool learning settings requires an integrated approach. In that regard, at the end of each chapter, we include a section titled "Tech Tips" listing developmentally appropriate ways of introducing and using technology to support children's engagement with play materials. Also punctuated throughout each chapter are sidebars titled "Now Try This!," which feature practical ideas and creative uses for select play materials.

At the end of each part, you will find a summary highlighting key points and questions encouraging you to reflect on your own life experiences and how your personal journey shapes the way you teach and interact with children.

Finally, there are two appendices to support preschool educators in their use of this book. **Appendix A** features a table that broadly describes the capabilities of children ages 3 through 5. **Appendix B**, which lists a collection of high-quality children's books, stems from our belief in the power of books to extend and encourage children's deeper engagement and connection with play materials.

PART ONE

· · · · · · · · · · · · · · · · ·

Essential Questions

The setting must promote not only children's learning but also their pleasure in learning and the motivation to pursue it. Because the classroom is a teacher's main work space, it should be welcoming and inspiring to the teacher, too.

—Ann S. Epstein, *The Intentional Teacher: Choosing the Best Strategies for Young Children's Learning,* Revised Edition

CHAPTER 1

Who?

Children from Ages 3 to 5

Children experience many developmental changes and milestones in the preschool years. They move from completely depending on others for their care to being able to express what they want and working toward getting it. Supportive teachers and developmentally appropriate environments enable children to thrive and reach their potential. The play materials chosen for the early learning setting support children as they discover the wonder of the world around them.

Preschool-age children take in the many experiences of their daily lives and try to make sense of them using the knowledge they have gained as infants and toddlers. As children grow, they formulate sophisticated ways of framing that knowledge and expanding on it. For example, while a toddler may find enjoyment and stimulation in filling and emptying a bucket, a younger preschooler might begin to see the bucket as a representation and wear it as a hat. An older preschooler further understands that the bucket has a purpose and that they may use it as a prop during pretend play scenarios.

Supporting the sometimes inconsistent development that occurs between the ages of 3 through 5 can be challenging. There can be wide developmental gaps between a 3-year-old and a 4-year-old and between a 4-year-old and a 5-year-old. Choosing the right play materials to support this age range means understanding the milestones of the developing child. It also means making sure that all learners feel comfortable and safe to explore, play, and learn. Rather than attaching milestones to a specific age, think of skill development as progressions

with a beginning, middle, and end. Acknowledge children's individual skill level and view each child as the unique being they are. This approach encourages teachers to take a broader, more holistic view of development.

As children grow, developmental milestones can guide teachers in their planning and interactions. These widely accepted developmental milestones are broad and geared toward children who are generally around the same age. However, progress through these developmental milestones is not a straight line and many children show growth in different areas at different rates. This can be due to many factors, including an innate giftedness in a learning and development domain, developmental delays or disabilities, culture, language, and personal experiences. Sometimes, teachers focus on the disability instead of the child and, as a result, do not provide the child with the same opportunities to be successful as their peers (Brillante 2018). For example, teachers might hold back certain play materials from a child with developmental delays or disabilities, rather than giving that child the opportunity to explore the materials and then modifying them as needed so that the child may engage with the materials in ways that are comfortable for them. Focus on what a child *can* do instead of what they cannot.

Cultural Considerations of Play and Play Materials

Throughout this section and in this book, the word *culture* is used in a broad sense. It is used not only to talk about race or ethnicity but also to refer to the social identities and dynamics of the children, families, and communities that make up each early learning program (Howard 2019).

Here are a few questions to consider when reflecting on the culture of the children you serve:

> What are the attitudes and goals of the community in which the children live?

> What are the values and practices within each child's home?

> How do these social identities and dynamics affect the way a child engages with play materials and integrates into the culture of your early learning setting?

Everything—a family's daily routines; who takes care of whom; where and when family members eat, sleep, and relax—impacts the way children participate in activities and routines in the early learning setting. Young children's exposure to play materials and their play experiences at home affect the way children engage in play at your program. For example, a child who throws blocks may not have previous experiences with those materials and therefore might not understand the expectations.

Deepa enters Ms. Owens's preschool class shortly after her third birthday. She often engages with many of the play materials in ways that are unexpected or even viewed as challenging by Ms. Owens, such as throwing items across the room and scribbling on the tables while laughing with delight.

Instead of getting angry or frustrated, Ms. Owens asks Deepa's mother about their family. She learns that Deepa's *naani* (maternal grandmother) has been her primary caregiver ever since Deepa's mother returned to work. They don't have many play materials in the small city apartment they all share, and Deepa has never seen so many colorful materials for building and drawing before coming to school! Deepa's mother also shares that one of the little girl's favorite things to do with her naani is to sing. They sing traditional songs from India and tunes from popular children's TV shows.

Ms. Owens is very glad to have the opportunity to learn this information—it explains so much about Deepa's behavior. After her talk with Deepa's mother, Ms. Owens comes up with ideas for engaging Deepa in activities that help her explore the new play materials appropriately. Knowing it is an interest for Deepa, she also plans to incorporate music into these interactions.

When observing how a child engages with a new material, ask yourself

› Has the child engaged with this material in a home or early learning setting before? If so, what were the expectations? Were they the same or different from yours?

› Has the child had enough time to explore the properties and possibilities of the material before being expected to use it the "right" way?

› Is the material appropriate for the child's developmental play stage?

Families' thoughts and feelings about play shape the experiences of the children in your setting. Consider a child with a tendency to wander away from the group. They may have difficulty following the rule of staying with the larger group, especially outdoors. The culture of their family may allow for—and even promote—more unsupervised play. On the other hand, children who tend to stay close to an adult or are hesitant to venture out on their own may be raised in a family where unsupervised self-directed play is discouraged or prevented by an adult who stays close by at all times. These opposing views of play shape the way a child integrates into the community of the early learning setting. When teachers commit to understanding and acknowledging diverse family relationships and practices, they can truly begin to take a multicultural perspective to working with children.

CHAPTER 2

Why?

Optimizing Learning, Development, and Well-Being

When supporting young children's learning and development, it is important to consider where, how, and with what young children play. Additionally, reflecting on *why* play is essential to how young children learn and how the materials in the learning environment support their development can provide insight into the best ways to extend children's learning. "Play is not frivolous: it enhances brain structure and function and promotes executive function (i.e., the process of learning, rather than the content), which allow us to pursue goals and ignore distractions" (Yogman et al. 2018, 1). Young children learn best when they are engaged in activities and experiences that are hands-on, relevant, and joyful and that provide opportunities for them to better understand the world (NAEYC 2022).

Preschoolers are not just future kindergartners—they are also former toddlers! As children move out of the toddler stage and into the preschool years, they enter one of the most expansive times of development. It's helpful to know about and consider children's previous experiences in an early learning setting to better understand the *why* behind certain behaviors. No matter how young, every child comes with stories and experiences that have shaped their development and approaches to learning. Maintaining open, honest, and reciprocal communication with families allows teachers to plan experiences and provide play materials curated for the children in their program. The play materials teachers curate for their early learning settings should be guided by the developmental domains as well as the interests of the

An Equitable Approach to Teaching and Learning

Asking and answering questions can be tricky when it comes to group time with 3- to 5-year-olds! Not every child will have the same ability or desire to answer a question you ask. Offering appropriate wait times to promote "thinking space" is an equitable approach to question-and-answer sessions with children. This can alleviate some of the pressure children might feel to perform quickly and enable them to give more authentic answers. The examples below offer a few ideas for how to intentionally invite children to engage in sharing their thoughts.

Instead of saying . . .	Consider saying . . .
"Quick! Who can answer my question first? Very good, Veda! You were first, you're so smart!"	"I'm going to ask you a question, but before you say something out loud, think about your answer until I ring this chime."
"Did you hear me? I asked you a question."	"Do you need another minute to think about your answer? Can I ask Andrei for his answer while you keep thinking?"
"You don't remember? We talked about this yesterday."	"I can tell by your face that you're still thinking about the answer. Let me know when you think of what you want to say. I'll be ready to listen!"

children. Often, the focus of teaching is on what children need to know (Wexler 2020). Think about why you include certain materials in your learning environment and how they support the growth of the whole child.

Here are a few helpful tips to keep in mind:

> Stay knowledgeable of the milestones in each domain of learning and development. Keep in mind that these milestones are broad general guidelines as each child learns and develops differently.

> Observe what play materials and areas of the learning environment children are drawn to in order to better understand where they are developmentally and how to scaffold children's thinking. Do they choose play materials that they can pretend with or materials they can construct with? Do they prefer areas with bright or muted colors? Do they shy away from noisy areas over quieter ones?

> Reflect often on how to extend children's interactions with play materials.

> Give children time to think and formulate their replies during conversations (Wasik & Hindman 2018). Taking a few seconds between asking your question and a child's response can provide you with insight into how the child processes information. (For more on this, see "An Equitable Approach to Teaching and Learning.")

Cognitive Learning and Development

During the early years, children's brains are making substantial cognitive gains (Mooney 2013). Preschoolers are developing conceptual knowledge of math, literacy, and science, and they seek new and creative ways to make sense of the information they have learned and how it can be applied in their daily life. They are interested in exploring their environment and determining how they can make connections. To support and encourage this learning and development, interactions and experiences with carefully curated play materials are key (New Jersey Department of Education 2015).

Preschool-age children are eager to learn and have an inherent desire to gather information. They may ask many questions as they seek to understand. When children ask questions, teachers can observe what children already know and use those observations to create new play experiences.

Focus your efforts on making the world accessible to them. Including real pots and pans in the dramatic play center, for example, builds a connection between the world that children see at home and the world they can interact with at school. Concepts such as shapes and colors should relate to materials, environments, and experiences with which the child is familiar. When learning about the color green, for example, instead of asking "What color is this?" you might consider the following questions and comments:

> "Where else do you see green in our classroom?"

> "What are some other things you can think of that are green?"

> "I see your grandma had on a green shirt on this morning. She must really like that color!"

Phrasing questions and comments in this intentional way builds a bridge between what the child is learning in a school setting and their real-world experiences. In this way, learning becomes relevant and meaningful to the child.

Consider how you can help children build their understanding of concepts through the play materials you provide that they engage with on a daily basis. For example, rather than memorizing the days of the week, help them to understand the passage of time in a way that relates to their lives. You might create calendars that count down the days to a special event or track the number of days they are engaged in a certain project, such as growing plants or hatching chicks.

Social and Emotional Learning and Development

In the early preschool years, children's verbal communication skills improve dramatically (Mooney 2018). As their vocabulary increases, so does their ability to identify their own emotions and the emotions of others as well as their ability to communicate with adults and peers (Joseph & Strain 2003). Preschoolers begin to consider the perspectives of others and listen to what their peers have to say. In doing so, they move toward an understanding that others might not have the same ideas as they do about an activity or play material they are engaging with. Invite children to talk about their viewpoints. Help mediate if persistent conflict arises when a child's ideas don't match those of another child.

You can also support children by modeling different interactions and problem-solving strategies:

> Model and encourage children to participate in conflict resolution steps, from gathering information to evaluating possible solutions.

> Create a neutral space (like a Peace Table) where children can go to calmly express their feelings and solve their problems.

> Engage children in making persona dolls that have their own identities and stories to tell. Use the dolls to help build children's emotional intelligence, recognizing the emotional needs of self and others (Whitney 2002).

> Share cue cards and charts with children that provide visual ways they can define their emotions and strategies to solve conflicts.

Physical Learning and Development

Preschoolers are made to move. They enjoy activities that encourage and allow for jumping, wiggling, dancing, and running. They need many different opportunities to discover how their bodies move in space (both indoors and outdoors) and how they can care for them. As children grow and mature, they gain greater control over the muscles in the body and can participate in complex movement patterns while developing strength and stamina (Goodway, Ozmun, & Gallahue 2019). Movement is essential to how children learn and process information; recent research has linked the positive effects of physical activity to language and mathematical abilities (de Waal 2019).

CHAPTER 3

How?

The Role of Teachers

Teachers have a critical role in choosing the "right stuff," but play materials alone cannot and do not support children's learning and development. As an early childhood educator, you know that in order for children to make meaning, your guidance is needed. This guidance happens as you set up and organize the learning environment, introduce and encourage exploration of play materials, observe children's play, and extend children's understanding through inquiry-based learning.

Setting Up and Organizing the Learning Environment

Everything teaches and everything matters. Whether you intend it to or not, how you present play materials *does* teach. If different types of materials are jumbled together, stacked carelessly, or in a different place every day, what message does that send to children? If marker caps are left off and paintbrushes remain unwashed and harden, what might the children learn about the treatment of materials?

Organizing the learning environment is key to providing a comfortable, inviting place for children to explore materials. You can arrange your space in ways that support children's developing independence and mobility. The arrangement should make sense to teachers *and* to the children. For example, a large, flat rug placed directly in front of the shelf where the unit blocks are stored supports and encourages construction, and it should be easy for children playing at the sand and water table to get to a nearby bin containing measuring cups, funnels, and shovels.

When considering the setup of your early learning setting, look at each learning center and ask yourself the following questions:

> Does the space support the type of play being encouraged by the materials?

> Can the play materials be used effectively in that space?

If there is a shopping cart and cash register in the dramatic play center, is there space to freely use those items without interrupting children who are using the housekeeping materials? If there are floor puzzles in the manipulatives center, is there a carpeted space to use them without needing to carry them to the block center?

Consider the word *accessibility* and what it looks like in your classroom. Most materials should be placed where children can access them without the teacher's help. For example, store manipulatives in open containers and arrange furniture with enough space for a child

Using the Early Learning Environment to Foster Independence and Self-Regulation

- **Label learning centers and play materials.** Creating labels for the different areas in your classroom and for new and popular play materials with the material's name and a photo promotes children's print awareness from both a reading and writing perspective (Pilonieta, Shue, & Kissel 2019). To support dual language learners (DLLs)—and to expose other children to languages other than English—include the name of the play material in the home languages of DLLs you teach (e.g., the English name in black and the Spanish name in green).

- **Organize play materials according to their use.** Group like things together so children have an easier time finding them. For example, the art center might have a Put Together shelf with tape, glue, staples and staplers, paper clips, and rubber bands and a Break Apart shelf with scissors and different kinds of hole punchers; the dramatic play center could separate materials for dress up from cooking materials; and the science center might have a balance scale and things to weigh placed together on a table.

- **Create a few rules for moving play materials in and out of various learning centers.** For example, children can bring river stones from the science center to the dramatic play center to use as vegetables for soup, but they must return the materials to their original places at cleanup time. Alternately, children can create a new collection of play materials gathered from around the room to use as "soup ingredients" in the future. Children can choose a space in the dramatic play center to store this new collection and create a label for it.

using a wheelchair to navigate around independently (Brillante 2017). When access to materials is blocked by another child using the space, some children may be too shy or not yet have the language to ask a classmate to move out of the way. For this reason, ensure that there are multiple access points to reach a material or plenty of room for children not to block each other while in the space.

The large volume of materials required in some preschool environments can seem overwhelming at times without a good organizational system in place. A lot of puzzles stacked up and pushed tightly into a shelf becomes an annoyance—or even a hazard—when children try to take one from the middle or bottom of the stack. In addition, most of these puzzles have now become impossible to use, just like the wonderful collections of art materials stuffed tightly onto a shelf. This way of storing materials does not allow children to independently take out materials, use them, and put them back without frustration or help. Think about how efficiently valuable shelf real estate is being used. Get into a routine of rotating materials to ensure that shelves do not become overcrowded and that children always have a blend of familiar and new play materials from which to choose.

At the beginning of the year or after changing something in the space midyear, an intentional introduction or review of the learning environment for children is key for establishing good housekeeping habits and routines. You might, for example, take children on a "train ride" around the room. In small groups, lead children around to the different areas of the room. Make a stop at each "station," or learning center. Point to the learning center sign, pick an item from the shelf, and ask, "What is this called?" or "What do you think this is?" Continue exploring the materials at that learning center and say, "Look at all of the different materials at this station. Is there a space here for you to work with these linking cubes?" Draw attention to the layout of the early learning setting. Point out the pathways, entrances, and exits of the learning center, and where children should use the materials found in that center.

As children interact with their environment, observe how they navigate through spaces. Follow through with questions and comments that bring attention to the different spaces and play materials. Here are some ideas for the kinds of questions you might ask:

> "Look at the picture and words on this container. Now look at the shelf. Can you match the labels?"

> "How can you design a label for this container so we know which toy to put in it?"

> "Where do you keep food at home? Where do you think would be a good place to store the food in our dramatic play center?"

> "Why do you think it's a good idea to put all the food in a separate box from the scarves?"

> "How do you feel when you go into the block center and it's a big mess? What can we do to solve that problem?"

> "How many of these big triangle blocks can fit in this container? Try putting away five rectangle blocks and I'll put away the cylinder blocks."

Involve children in both the successes and challenges of the environment. When you see a child wipe the table after they've used watercolors, you might comment, "Thank you for cleaning up your spill! Now the table won't get stained from the paint." Or when you notice a child putting

Ideas for Involving Children in Organizing and Caring for the Early Learning Environment

- **Making outlines of play materials for use during cleanup.** One system for cleanup that provides children with visual guidance for where to store items (and promotes one-to-one correspondence!) is creating paper outlines of specific materials and placing them around the room. Have children carefully trace play materials onto colorful construction paper; cut them out; and affix the outlines with tape or putty to the shelf, wall, or hook where the specific material it represents belongs. (This works well for materials such as cooking utensils in the dramatic play center, unit blocks in the block center, clipboards in the writing center, and magnifying glasses in the science center.) While creating the outlines, you might give younger preschoolers cues like "Try and keep the pencil touching the edge of the wooden spoon while you go around it," or offer support by holding and turning the paper while a child manipulates the scissors. Older preschoolers can write the name of the material directly on the outline cutouts either by using invented spellings or copying words from a piece of paper you provide.

- **Sweeping and cleaning spills.** To support children's self-help skills and instill good cleanup habits, provide cleaning tools for children to access and use, such as a small handheld brush and dustpan or vacuum near the sand table and paper or cloth towels near the water table. Spills are often accidental, but sometimes they are the result of an excited preschooler who is discovering cause and effect by splashing in the water table or wondering how much milk will fit into their cup. Teach children that the cleanup process can be just as fun and rewarding as the play itself.

- **Assigning classroom helper jobs.** On a rotating basis, give children designated roles for cleanup. For example, the librarian neatly arranges books on the shelf, the building manager makes sure that unit blocks are put away according to the shape outlines on the shelf, the house inspector checks that dramatic play materials are put away properly, and the sensory table supervisor sweeps and wipes up any sand or water left on the floor. This is also an authentic way to introduce rich vocabulary relating to communities and jobs. (For a more in-depth discussion of classroom helper jobs, see Chapter 10.)

unit blocks away after using them, say, "You've really helped the classroom community stay neat. Your friends who come in here next will have a nice clean space to work!" If children aren't meeting your expectations for cleanup, talk with them about it. You might ask, "How could we solve the problem of the collage materials always falling on the floor in the art center?" Involving children in the care of their learning space not only teaches self-help skills and a sense of community, it also makes your day-to-day job less stressful!

The physical environment also communicates to children expectations for how to interact with other people and the learning setting itself. Teachers who struggle with classroom management often have classrooms with disorganized or poorly maintained materials. They get frustrated with children who do not clean up or who have trouble paying attention. Many times, behaviors like these occur because the materials children are using are incomplete or broken (Harms, Clifford, & Cryer 2014). Craft sticks are left on the table or dropped on the floor because they don't have a labeled space on the shelf, or a child loses interest in a collage project because all the glue bottles are dried or empty. When the learning environment and its contents are well organized, teachers can spend less time helping children access materials and managing their behavior and more time interacting and observing. Early learning settings where children depend on the teacher for frequent help and direct instruction to use materials create challenges for both teachers and children. Reflect on the organization of your learning environment, the materials available, and how it affects the climate of your space and how children are learning.

Introducing and Encouraging Exploration of Play Materials

Just as young children's relationships with each other take time to develop, so do their relationships with play materials. Not all children have the same level of experience or ability with different types of play materials.

> Three-year-old Noelle enters preschool with a lot of experience using art materials. Her parents love art, and they often paint and draw with her at home. Due to her many experiences with tools like paintbrushes and chalk, Noelle has well-developed fine motor skills. However, materials for building are new to her. Her teachers support her as she explores them for the first time and develops the coordination needed to do things like create sturdy block towers.

Whether or not a play material is familiar or new to a child, there should always be an exploration period when the child can discover the properties, functions, and features of the play material on their own. This period of relationship building is necessary in order for children to eventually engage with play materials in more complex ways. When bringing a new material into your early learning setting, invite children to touch, arrange, and connect with it for some time. For example, before preschoolers can sort, pattern, and create structures with shapes, they need the time and space to play with shapes by exploring play materials like blocks—seeing the colors and feeling the edges, corners, and curves. After plenty of experiences with blocks, older preschoolers are well on their way to engaging with them in more complicated ways, such as breaking apart shapes into several smaller shapes (*decomposing*) and learning new related vocabulary, such as *semicircle, isosceles triangle*, and *trapezoid* (Turrou, Johnson, & Franke 2021). These relationships with play materials develop over time, and the exploration period should be honored and built into any expectation or assessment early childhood teachers might have for each child.

There are several ways you can approach introducing new play materials to children:

> **Small or whole group time.** Bring a small group of children to a table or to the learning center where the play material is stored. Alternately, gather the whole group together at your circle time rug or area. If possible, pass out the material so that each child has one to explore. Once the children have spent some time with the material, ask some probing questions ("What colors [shapes] do you see?," "What else can you tell me about this?," "What are some ways you think we can use this?").

> **Think, pair, share.** After handing children a new play material, give them a few moments to explore it. Then invite children to turn to the child next to them and share their thoughts about the material. This approach may be difficult for younger preschoolers with limited communication skills; however, older preschoolers should be able to understand what is being asked and engage in a conversation with a peer. Move around the group to listen in on what children are saying to gain a better understanding of what they already know and what they are struggling with. Bring the group back together and encourage each pair to share something they talked about with the whole group. (Note: Avoid choosing the child who will share; rather, let the children take ownership and choose for themselves.)

> **Choice time.** After placing a new play material in the learning center, spend time in that area to be on hand when children discover it to observe and facilitate their play as needed. "Becoming skillful at using a *few* open-ended toys in many different ways can lead children to more productive play in the long run [. . .] however, keep in mind that some children will need your help, at least initially, to figure out what to do with them and to find interesting problems to work on with them" (Levin 2013, 87).

> **Element of surprise.** During whole group time, display a picture of the play material or the material itself and ask the children to go on a scavenger hunt to find it in the early learning environment. You can also introduce a featured material box or jar (Strasser & Bresson 2017). Create a colorful, inviting container that the children cannot see into. When you're ready to introduce a new play material, place it in the container out of children's sight. Shake and move it around to create suspense and interest, and ask children questions ("What do you hear when I shake the container?," "What do you think might be inside?"). Reveal the item inside and let the children know that it is a new material for their classroom. Challenge them to look for it during choice time.

When introducing a new play material, observe children's play, document what you see and hear, and ask open-ended questions. Questions such as "Tell me what this looks (feels, sounds) like" give you an idea of what kind of vocabulary the child knows to describe the material. This is an excellent time to introduce rich, descriptive words, such as *twinkly, nubby, itty bitty, round*, and *wobbly*. Often, children have already been exposed to more robust vocabulary without realizing it. For example, a child who has sung the song "Twinkle, Twinkle, Little Star" repeatedly might be able to recite the words from memory. However, consider whether that child knows what the word *twinkle* represents. Have they held something that *twinkles*? Has a teacher helped to make the connection between the word and what *twinkling* actually looks like in play materials they use in the classroom?

Mr. Asqueri's preschool classroom has prisms hanging in one of its many windows. The children are fascinated by the refraction of light when the sun shines through the prisms. "This prism is so twinkly!" Mr. Asqueri exclaims. "That's when something looks like its blinking and shining because the light is bouncing off it. Do you see anything else in our classroom that twinkles? Have you ever heard the word *twinkle* before?"

If a child is not able to make the connection between vocabulary and concrete materials from their daily life right away, you might scaffold their understanding through thoughtful conversation or questions ("Hmm . . . I wonder if you've ever heard the word *twinkle* in a story or a song before"). If they still do not make the connection, leave the conversation alone and allow the exploration of the prisms to continue. Remind the child, "Listen for that word today. Maybe it will pop up somewhere!" After making that comment, of course be sure to sing "Twinkle, Twinkle Little Star" with the class later in the day!

As part of the introduction process, talk with children about how to find the play material once it is incorporated into their environment, where they might use it comfortably, and how to clean it up. Above all, be patient and enthusiastic. The more excited you are about a new material, the more likely children will be ready and willing to engage with it. This introduction and exploration period will tell you much about each child's approach to learning, developmental progression, and understanding of the concepts the play material promotes.

Observing Children's Play

While it is critical to offer consistent guidance for children's behavior with and use of materials, it is also important to know when to step back and simply watch (Tapia, Pickering, & Coffino 2021). Observation in your early learning setting has many benefits. This section focuses specifically on what observation can tell you about your learning environment and the play materials you offer.

Observing children starts with paying attention to how each child learns, behaves, and reacts to new situations or materials and how they interact with their peers. Children's understanding of and interest in play materials can look different from week to week (Jones 2018). To guide your observations of children's play with materials, consider these questions:

> What play materials are children drawn to the most? Do they gravitate toward items that are new to them (e.g., mirrored prisms, Magna-Tiles), that they may not usually be "allowed" to play with (e.g., funnels, turkey basters), or that are very familiar to them (e.g., LEGO bricks, dolls)?

> Are there play materials some children get easily frustrated with? Are these materials too simple or too advanced for those children?

> What play materials do children seem to ignore? What might be some of the reasons?

> Are there enough visually interesting and tactile play materials? Are they open ended?

> Are children using play materials in the same way over and over again, or do they seem to approach materials in a variety of ways?

> How are children using the space where a play material is stored? Do they seem crowded and unfocused? Is there plenty of space to play without interruption?

You will notice a lot if you listen to what children like and why. A child may explore many different play materials in the learning environment but always seems to go back to the same type of materials; for example, a child who frequently gravitates toward the unit blocks or LEGO bricks or one who enjoys the geometric quality of shape stencils, rulers, and shape sorters. It's important to remember that children's "preferences are a sign of their own personality growth and the emerging peer relationships that become exceedingly important as they mature" (Auerbach 2012). Reflect on the information gathered during observations and how it can help you improve your early learning setting to meet the needs of your preschoolers.

Play materials can be rotated in and out based on what you observe about the children's developing skills and interests. When rotating materials, teachers can

> Share play materials with other teachers

> Access any extra items their program may have or that were set aside in storage

> Incorporate play materials that children collect outdoors or that children's families donate

Observing children at play also allows you to assess how materials might be affecting the social climate of your classroom. For example, if children are frequently fighting over materials, it could mean there aren't enough interesting things to do or there aren't enough of the most popular materials. If children struggle with turn-taking, it could mean that you need to offer more play materials and activities where children work together.

Show a genuine curiosity and wonder for children's discoveries. Ultimately, teachers want children to know that learning feels good. When the climate of an early learning setting encourages expression in many forms, children feel confident in their work and what they know. They feel safe knowing that it's okay to experiment with ideas and materials, to fail, and to try again.

Extending Children's Understanding Through Inquiry-Based Learning

There are many words to describe *inquiry-based learning*—projects, themes, investigations. Creating an environment and classroom culture that encourage children to wonder, ask questions, and seek answers are at the core of this approach. Child-centered, long-term studies are opportunities for children to decide what material or topic they want to know about and then lead an investigation to explore it. Offering interesting materials that spark young children's curiosity and appeal to their senses encourages children to want to know more. Children set out on the path of discovery and become active participants in their own learning.

Three- to 5-year-olds are naturally curious, but they may need support in learning how to ask questions. They need to feel safe to wonder and explore. Teachers can respond to these inquiries and plan activities based on what children want to know. To fully grasp what children want to learn, teachers need to move away from what they themselves are interested in and become immersed in what the children respond to. With this mindset, any time becomes the right time to capitalize and build on children's curiosity.

The children in Ms. Van Dyne's mixed-age preschool classroom sit at their small group lunch table discussing the seeds they found in their apple slices.

"The *semillas* (seeds), they need water to grow! Right, Ms. Van Dyne?" comments 4-year-old Roberto. The classroom's science and discovery center always has collections of seeds available in small baskets that children frequently discuss. Roberto has some understanding of how things grow.

Instead of saying "Yes, that's right! Good job, Roberto," Ms. Van Dyne wonders out loud, "Hmm. Why do they need water? Why not juice or milk?" Roberto looks away and shrugs his shoulders, unsure of how to answer. "How do you think we could figure that out?" Ms. Van Dyne prompts further. Even when no one makes a guess, instead of answering the question and shutting down lines of inquiry, she gives the children time to think and wonder for themselves.

The following morning, Ms. Van Dyne adds soil, pots, seeds, a juice box, a small carton of milk, a squeeze bottle of vinegar, and a spray bottle of water to the science and discovery center. She mentions casually at morning meeting, "There are some new materials in the science center today. You should check it out!" She does not bring the children together to watch as she demonstrates placing the seeds and soil in pots and pouring the liquids over them. Rather, she observes as the children who led the previous day's discussion make their way to the science and discovery center. As the children investigate the materials, she listens as they describe what they see and come up with ideas about how to use them.

"These are seeds from our apple. We need to put them in water," says 4-year-old Yasmin.

Three-year-old Isaias, who eagerly participated in the previous day's conversation, comments on the different liquids on the table. "I'm gonna put the milk for mine."

Ms. Van Dyne takes a backseat and lets the children drive the conversation. She answers questions like "How much milk do we put in?" and "How do you open the juice?," but she encourages the children to guide the experiment. Her openness to possibilities allows the children to feel comfortable sharing and testing their ideas.

To expand the investigation, Ms. Van Dyne includes other materials that relate to the apple seed study like books about seeds, tweezers, seeds of different sizes and varieties, and small pots labeled with numbers to count seeds into. She also created a class graph to gather children's predictions about how the seeds will grow. Over the next few weeks, the group's interest in the project ebbs and flows. Some children move from closely watching the apple seed pots every day to checking out the other collections of seeds on the shelf.

As the seed project continues, Ms. Van Dyne encourages the children to think of solutions or changes to their experiment. When it becomes clear that the plant being given milk is not growing and in fact starts to produce an odor, she encourages the children to record the results in journals.

A successful inquiry-based project for young children is when they are not worried about whether an answer is wrong or right or whether a question is good or bad. It's when children are given the freedom to construct ideas and knowledge as they explore. This book defines *constructing knowledge* as creating an understanding of a concept based on information children are told, things children experience firsthand, and things children express. During the apple seed study, the children in Ms. Van Dyne's class were exposed to all three. Rather than simply repeating information or facts that were "right" or "wrong," the children created an understanding of what was happening through a meaningful experience and came up with ways to communicate that knowledge, forming new connections and ideas during the process of hands-on learning and communicating. At the end of the apple seed project, except for one sprout, nothing grew. Yet the children were exposed to a way of thinking that gave them the comfort and flexibility to take chances despite their outcomes.

Early childhood educators face a real challenge: helping children achieve certain educational goals while simultaneously meeting professional goals themselves. Allowing inquiry-based learning to happen requires feeling comfortable enough in your own skills of inquiry as a

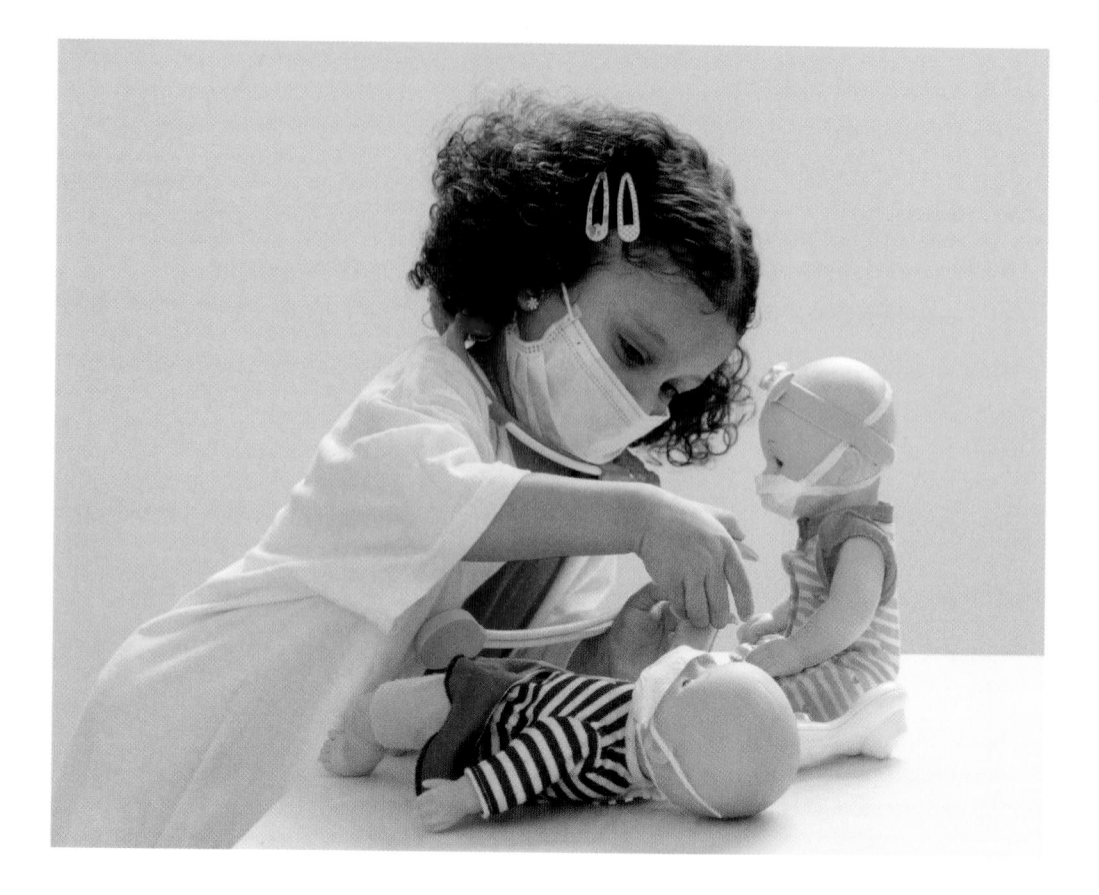

teacher and confident enough in children's growing abilities. If you haven't tried it before, it can be difficult releasing control over a project. You may find yourself saying, "But I don't have a lesson plan for that!" This sometimes causes anxiety that inquiry-based learning or child-directed activities won't work. Our advice to you is to take the leap!

When children express interest in a certain topic or material, let that be your guide for what to study next. It can be something as complex as building and figuring out how robots work or as simple as a few apple seeds discovered at lunchtime. Begin by incorporating one child-directed activity into your lesson planning or presenting a new play material and seeing what the children can teach *you* with it. A variety of well-chosen materials will often lead you to new, more authentic methods of assessing and understanding children's abilities. Consider the many uses of materials and the ways they can be used to meet child assessment needs and performance standards.

Developing a set of questions you can ask children during an inquiry-based study can also help prepare you for the unexpected directions that children's curiosity may take you. Consider these topics for lines of questioning and exploration of a play material:

> Physical (e.g., shape, color, texture, size)

> Sensory (e.g., touch, sight, feel, smell, sound)

> Mechanical (e.g., how things move, how things are built)

> Perspective (e.g., how things look from different angles, how things changes over time)

The comments you make and the questions you ask should reinforce children's current knowledge but also support their next phase of development. Be prepared to respond to their needs and guide them but also be willing to step back. Look at the way you approach exploration of materials and interactions with the children you teach. Ask yourself, "Am I telling the children what they need to know, or am I guiding them to discover the answers for themselves?" It is important to have a balance between teacher- and child-directed activities, and children's interests are a valuable source of insight for activity planning and choosing play materials. Intentional teachers respond to those interests and are eager to join children on the journey.

Everything children wonder about is important. A certain play material, activity, or idea might be significant to the child for reasons that aren't immediately apparent. If you are unsure of how to determine what to focus on for an inquiry-based study, start with careful observations of the children. Listen closely to what they are saying when they engage with materials and while they talk to their peers. Wonder about things out loud, and create a space where children feel empowered to do the same.

CHAPTER 4

What?

Play Materials for Preschoolers

Play materials for preschoolers can take many forms. Sometimes, a play material is a complex building kit purchased from an expensive store. Other times, it is the container from a pint of strawberries. Often, play materials fall somewhere in between this scope. The availability of time, space, play materials, and playmates all have a role in how preschoolers approach play and play materials (Gosso & Almeida Carvalho 2013).

Defining What Play Materials Are

Play materials for preschool children are **toys, resources**, and **everyday objects** that support the development of children's cognitive, social and emotional, and physical skills.

Toys: Objects that children use to play (e.g., dolls, manipulatives, musical instruments, unit blocks)

Resources: Objects that are not categorized as toys but do enhance and extend play (e.g., art materials, books, classroom rules charts, restaurant menus)

Everyday objects: Objects that are found in, repurposed from, or relevant to what children may see in their everyday lives (e.g., acorns, empty food boxes, plastic cups, twigs)

What do these play materials have in common? They are fun, interesting, flexible, and developmentally appropriate materials that engage preschoolers in active learning and promote their development as well as their well-being. They offer children of varying ages and abilities the opportunity to construct knowledge. Focused on preschool children ages 3 through 5, many of the play materials and ideas suggested throughout this book are also appropriate for children transitioning in and out of preschool: older toddlers and younger kindergarteners.

It is important to note that the play materials suggested in this book are not absolute, nor do you need to have each and every one available all the time. They are suggestions rather than prescriptive guidelines. There is much room for creative interpretation within each material and skill being addressed. Also, since children's interests and ideas should be appreciated and honored, there are many opportunities for crossover within each learning and development domain.

Selecting Play Materials

Choosing the "right stuff" is rarely as simple as it seems. Preschool settings should offer play materials that not only support children's cognitive, social and emotional, and physical learning and development but also meet the unique needs and interests of each child (NAEYC 2022).

As previously discussed, young children develop at different rates, sometimes making it difficult to know how to support each individual child. Providing play materials that support children at their varying levels of development and are engaging and interesting enough to maintain children's sense of enjoyment is an excellent place to start. Materials, whether purchased, created, or found, come together in the early learning setting to provide an environment that makes children eager to learn (NAEYC 2022).

Most early childhood educators are familiar with

> **Open-ended materials**, or materials that do not have a predetermined, "right or wrong" way of being used or fixed properties (e.g., blocks, paint, sand, water, playdough)

> **Close-ended materials**, or materials that do have a predetermined way of being used, which a child either can or cannot do (e.g., puzzles, board games, shape sorters)

Consider these different types of materials and how each best supports the children you teach. A mix of open- and close-ended materials are suitable for all learners. The right combination of materials also provides opportunities for teachers to scaffold what children know and help them extend their capabilities. As subsequent chapters discuss, scaffolding plays an important role in supporting children's learning.

When observing the play materials a child prefers, ask yourself questions like the following to help you understand why:

> If a child prefers more close-ended materials and activities, what is it about the materials that they find enjoyable? Do the materials make them feel safe and successful? Do they enjoy repeating the same task over and over? What does this potentially say about the child's needs, particularly their emotional needs?

> If a child prefers more open-ended materials and activities, do they have a plan or end result in mind for their play? If so, what are they choosing to represent through these open-ended materials and activities? Have they had previous exposure to the materials at home or in another learning setting?

Over time, children's interest in specific play materials might ebb and flow. This can be due to their familiarity with the material, the current focus of interest in the setting, or that children have developed skills beyond the materials you currently have accessible. When it seems as though children's interest in a material has waned, consider what you might do to reignite interest. Some ideas include

> **Changing the location.** Moving a collection of river stones or shells from the science center to the dramatic play center can inspire children to consider them in a new light. The stones they were so intent on sorting by size and color in the science center might become ingredients in the lasagna they are making! While interacting with a child using the play material, draw their attention to the properties of the material and see where the conversation leads you.

> **Changing the way a play material is displayed.** Take the bin of long-forgotten foam dice from the bottom shelf of the manipulatives center and place them on top of the shelf. You might display them on an unbreakable mirror or inside a clear container that children can view from all sides. Place some extension materials, such as textured numbers or counting bears, next to them. This allows children to see how different materials can be connected and combined.

> **Putting the play material away for a rainy day.** If changing things around doesn't do the trick, put the material in storage for a while and bring it out the following month. Materials that sit on a shelf untouched for several weeks or months should be reevaluated. Be sure to rotate in a new material for anything that is removed.

Materials also need to be chosen with respect for the children who play with them. The children and families you serve should see themselves reflected in the play materials you offer. Include materials like dolls, books, and playsets that represent many shades of skin, hair, and eye color. Incorporate materials that recognize and welcome children with diverse family structures (e.g., single parents, parents who are different races, families with adopted children, LGBTQIA+ families). Similarly, your learning setting should feature play materials that represent people with varying abilities and that challenge stereotypes and norms, including those related to gender, race, age, and ability. Play materials that represent a broad range of cultures, abilities, races, languages, classes, genders, and other identities help children understand differences and similarities among themselves and their families. Exposure to these inclusive materials, accompanied by thoughtful interactions, helps children challenge what is often misrepresented on television and in other media.

Safety Considerations

Authentic and engaging preschool learning settings can never be completely free of all potential hazards. The third edition of the *Early Childhood Environmental Rating Scale* (ECERS-3) states that a safe space is one where risk of severe injury is substantially diminished. The observation tool acknowledges that a hazard in one situation may not be in another and advises teachers to weigh the safety of play materials and environments through the lens of "the nature of the supervision, the characteristics of the children in the group, or the amount of exposure to the hazard" (Harms, Clifford, & Cryer 2014, 34). Using their knowledge of developmentally appropriate practice, child development, and widely accepted resources on safety, teachers can make informed choices about the materials to include in their early learning settings.

Physical Safety

The US Consumer Product Safety Commission (CPSC), ASTM International's Standard Consumer Safety Specification for Toy Safety, and the Underwriters Laboratories Toy Safety Certification Mark are useful resources when determining whether a play material is safe. According to the CPSC, safe toys for young children are generally those that are free of obvious causes of harm. These guidelines include the following:

> No sharp edges or points

> Lack of very small parts

> No long cords that can become entangled

> Use of nontoxic and lead-free paints or components

> Being constructed with durability and ease of cleaning in mind (CPSC, n.d.)

Check play materials regularly to ensure that they are in good working order and broken parts and pieces are removed.

When considering the physical safety of play materials, remember that you know the children best. What you choose to include in the learning environment should reflect that understanding, and it should also factor in the child's current developmental level and ability (Harms, Clifford, & Cryer 2014). For example, some children you teach may be prone to mouthing objects; therefore, the play materials you provide should minimize the potential for choking hazards. The better you know the children in your care, the better able you will be to select safe and appropriate play materials.

Consider, too, your own comfort and familiarity with a new play material before introducing it to the early learning setting. Take time to experiment and play with the material yourself before sharing it with the children. At first, the idea of including real hammers and nails may seem overwhelming; however, if you take time to experiment with strategies on how to work with children to hold the nail or swing the hammer, you can find your comfort level and share your new discovery with the children. That said, if the idea of bringing hammers and nails into your setting gives you too much pause, move on and try something else.

Appropriate Content

Choosing safe materials is not limited to how they are made; it is also critical to make sure that play materials send positive, bias-free social messages and do not expose children to content for which they are not emotionally or psychologically ready (NAEYC 2019). For example, many young children are familiar with popular contemporary songs targeted to adult audiences, even though the language and concepts are not always appropriate. It can be difficult to find a balance between what children have heard outside of the learning setting and what is actually appropriate. If this kind of music seems to be a motivator for the children you teach, the music brand Kidz Bop reworks and covers chart-topping songs to make the lyrics more child friendly. Be sure to give the songs a listen before using them with children, just in case.

Many teachers incorporate books and music from their own childhoods, not always knowing their origins or realizing the biases they contain. Books like *The Cat in the Hat* (by Dr. Seuss) and songs like "Do Your Ears Hang Low?" were originally penned with biases. It's difficult to know the history of every book you read or song you sing with children, but it is important to not continue the culture of bias that exists in some of these historical media. Branch out and consider books that feature characters of color or that share stories from diverse perspectives, such as *The Proudest Blue* (by Ibtihaj Muhammad, with S.K. Ali, illustrated by Hatem Aly) and *Jabari Jumps* (by Gaia Cornwall). You can look for book lists and reviews on websites such as www.teachingforchange.org or www.diversebooks.org, both of which curate lists of high-quality literature that support equity. Explore instrumental pieces and more current children's musicians, such as Jack Hartmann (www.jackhartmann.com) and Patty Shukla (www.pattysprimarysongs.com), that encourage children to respond to the tone and tempo of the music.

Online Concerns

Technology is a bigger part of children's lives than it ever has been, and children are more tech-savvy too; however, not all of what is available and labeled for children online is appropriate. When using devices that can access the internet, demonstrate for young children effective online research skills. Working with a well-curated list of websites or search parameters is key when going online with children, but there are several child-friendly search engines that might also be used:

> **Kiddle** (www.kiddle.co) is a visual search engine with web, image, and video search results that are continuously monitored by editors.

> **Teach the Children Well** (www.teachthechildrenwell.com) is a directory of websites, carefully curated by a teacher with inclusion and children's safety in mind, on a wide variety of topics.

As early childhood educators, it is easy to get wrapped up in the many concerns over health and safety requirements, learning standards, benchmarks, and assessments. However, it is important to remember the effectiveness of providing authentic experiences with play materials, playing with and becoming a thought partner to the child, and following children on their learning journey. The importance of discovering joy must not be forgotten.

Summary and Reflection

Asking yourself these essential questions—who, why, how, and what—is an important first step in curating play materials for the children you teach. There are many aspects to consider and rarely is there a one-size-fits-all approach. The need to remain an educator who is self-reflective and intentional increases as communities continue to shift and the field of early childhood education evolves and professionalizes. Rumenapp, Morales, and Lykouretzos (2018, 73) point out that "as early childhood education becomes more accessible to all families, teachers welcome children with wider ranges of abilities and of cultural and linguistic backgrounds," reminding educators both of this shifting landscape and of the necessity to remain flexible, open minded, and inclusive of all young learners.

. . . .

Now Ask Yourself This

- Think about your childhood, family, and cultural values. How has your upbringing shaped the way you work and play?

- What are some things you think you are good at? How did you gain and improve on those skills?

- What stops you from pursuing certain interests?

- What kinds of materials, activities, or places inspire you to learn and create?

- Recall a time when you had a breakthrough in your own learning or skill development. How did it feel? How does it feel when the children you teach have one of these "aha!" moments?

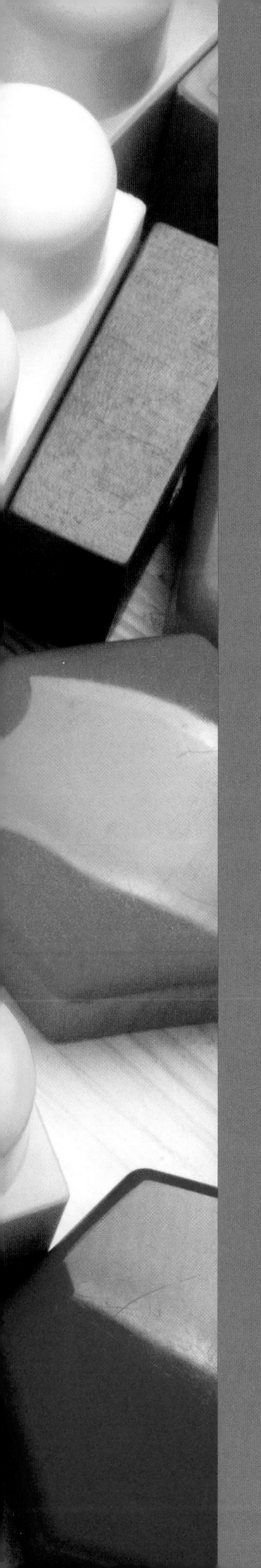

PART TWO

Cognitive Learning and Development

Learning and teaching should not stand on opposite banks and just watch the river flow by; instead, they should embark together on a journey down the water. Through an active, reciprocal exchange, teaching can strengthen learning how to learn.

—Loris Malaguzzi, as quoted in *The Hundred Languages of Children: The Reggio Emilia Approach—Advanced Reflections*, Second Edition, edited by Carolyn Edwards, Lella Gandini, and George Forman

Suggested Play Materials

Identifying Letters and Their Sounds

- Alphabet playdough mats, stampers (uppercase and lowercase letters), and playdough
- Letter cards and stencils
- Magnetic boards and letter magnets

Writing and Print Awareness

- Bookmaking supplies (e.g., cardboard and cardstock; hole punchers; interesting paper, such as construction paper, scrapbook paper, wallpaper samples, and wrapping paper; yarn and staplers for binding)
- Chalkboards and chalk
- Craft or recycled materials for forming letter shapes (e.g., chenille stems, coffee stirrers, craft sticks, Wikki Stix)
- Dry-erase boards and markers
- Paper of various kinds and sizes (e.g., easel pads, notepads, sticky notes, wallpaper samples, wrapping paper)
- Print materials (e.g., circulars, magazines, menus from a wide variety of restaurants, toy catalogs)
- Trays with sand or finger paint
- Writing utensils of various thickness (e.g., crayons, colored pencils and pens, highlighters, felt-tip markers)

Storytelling, Listening, and Comprehension

- Books in various formats (e.g., audio, e-book, print) and languages (e.g., Braille, children's home languages, wordless)
- Felt board and felt pieces
- Puppets
- Story baskets containing a variety of unrelated found, store-bought, and handmade items

CHAPTER 5

Play Materials That Support My Language and Literacy Skills

Both thoughtfully chosen literacy materials and your interactions with children support the learning and development of important reading, writing, and communication skills (Pilonieta, Shue, & Kissel 2019). This chapter highlights play materials that support the development of the following skills:

❯ Identifying letters and their sounds

❯ Writing and the awareness of print and its purposes

❯ Storytelling, listening, and comprehension

Play materials that support language and literacy encourage children to understand and use conventions of spoken, signed, and written communication. They can build on children's interests and experiences, introduce new vocabulary and ideas, or encourage children to become authors of their own story. These play materials can be bought, made, or found, and they are often dependent on the interactions teachers provide while children use them.

> Five-year-old Rey enters his classroom on Monday morning, excited to share the details of his Saturday afternoon adventure at the supermarket with his *abuela* (grandmother). When he mentions it to his teacher, Ms. Phillipa, she exclaims, "Tell me all about it!" As Rey describes the visit, Ms. Phillipa's head is swimming with ideas for incorporating his real-life experience into the classroom. She uses Rey's story as an opportunity to expand his vocabulary and support his communication skills. When Rey describes the "money taker" who helped him and his grandmother at checkout, his teacher introduces the vocabulary word *cashier*. Ms. Phillipa decides

to add supermarket props such as circulars, empty food boxes provided by families, and a toy cash register to the dramatic play center. She also plans to encourage Rey to create his own grocery store circular to practice his writing skills and letter sounds.

Engaging with young children while they use literacy materials provides opportunities for expanding listening and comprehension skills, supporting rich vocabulary development, and infusing writing and print awareness. While it is important to think about how to effectively scaffold children's learning and development in these areas, it is equally as important to consider the child's current developmental stage. Comments and questions like "Tell me more" and "What else can you tell me about that?" encourage children to think more deeply and communicate their thoughts, but some children—including young 3-year-olds, children with language delays, or children learning multiple languages—need more wait time before they are ready to offer a reply (Strasser & Bresson 2017). If a child struggles to answer a question or contribute to a conversation, add hand gestures or use play materials as supports to help the child understand what you are saying. Be patient and allow for a child to take as much time as they need to reply. To further encourage communication when a child is having difficulty articulating verbally, ask the child to show you what they mean by using their hands or pointing to a material.

Language is an ever-evolving skill for young children. It is a learned form of communication that is carefully scaffolded as children develop. Provide interesting play materials that spark their interest and inspire them to communicate, listen, express, and explore.

Trays with Sand or Finger Paint

Because preschool-age children are mostly concrete thinkers, abstract materials like alphabet charts, toys covered in letters, or the ABC song alone are not enough to fully support their developing literacy skills. Hands-on letter learning is the way to go! Plastic trays with one- to two-inch-deep sides or shallow aluminum pans are great tools children can use to explore letter formation. Make trays accessible for children to use independently during self-directed play. If you are concerned about spills, you might use pencil boxes, which can be closed between uses.

Many younger preschoolers enjoy the feeling of dragging their fingers through the sand and watching lines and shapes form. For different sensory experiences, you might vary the material placed in the tray, such as shaving cream or soil. Observe the children's fine motor dexterity and, as needed, support them by modeling how to curl their fingers into their palm and drag an index finger through the sand. Encourage children to experiment with creating and combining different types of lines, curves, and angles ("I see you made a straight line; I wonder how we can make a different type of line"). Model curved, notched, and zigzag lines, commenting how certain lines look like letters ("Oh my goodness! This zigzag line you made looks like the letter Z!"). Children with sensory sensitivities might be reluctant to touch the sand. For these children, consider what accommodations and modifications you can put in place, such as changing out the materials for ones they prefer or having nonlatex disposable gloves available for use.

As children become more familiar with this exploratory form of scribbling, drawing, and writing, add handwritten or printed letter cards alongside the trays to encourage letter formation. Here are a few ways you can use these letter cards:

> Invite children to reproduce the letters they see on the cards.

> Name the letters on the cards and encourage children to repeat and/or identify the letter names.

> Encourage the awareness of letter–sound connections ("I want to find and make the letter that makes the /t/ sound. Can you help me?").

Older preschoolers with more fine motor control may be interested in using craft sticks, paintbrushes, spoons, or other tools to create letters in the sand. Remember the diversity of children in your early learning setting and include letters and characters used in the writing systems of their home languages (e.g., Arabic, Cyrillic, Japanese). When children feel comfortable recognizing and naming letters, encourage them to write sight words or use invented spelling to write vocabulary words based on the classroom unit of study.

Books and Bookmaking Supplies

There are many benefits of reading books with children, including positive behavior implications, more rapid brain development, exposure to high-level vocabulary, and strong social connections (Trelease & Giorgis 2019). High-quality books with interesting and appealing illustrations grab children's attention and encourage them to pick up those books to look at the pictures and the words. The books in your early learning setting should reflect the diversity of the children, families, and communities you serve (e.g., different races, genders, ages, abilities, customs) as well as familiar activities, experiences, and events (Wanless & Crawford with Friedman 2020). Avoid choosing books that feature stereotypes. Display books on low bookshelves with their covers visible. If you have a hardcover book with an illustrated dust jacket and plain cover underneath, using contact paper will attach it to the book for visual appeal while also protecting it and reducing wear and tear. Include books in *every* learning center relating to each center's intended play focus, not just the literacy center. (See Appendix B for a list of children's books recommendations that connect to the learning and development domains explored in Parts Two through Four.)

Observe how children engage with books when they enter your early learning setting for the first time. You may see children holding books upside down or backward. You may see them holding the book right-side up or turning several pages at a time. They may comment on the illustrations they see or even invent their own story. Focus your initial efforts on book-handling skills. Support children by engaging in frequent read-alouds, modeling holding a book right-side up, and turning the pages from right to left. You might comment on or describe what you are seeing and doing ("I want to see the pictures right-side up," or "I'm turning one page at a time; I want to see what comes next").

When introducing a new book to children, read the story from beginning to end without interruptions. This allows the children to immerse in the magic of the story and the way illustrations interact with the text (Strasser & Bresson 2017). After the initial reading, ask children to describe what they see on the pages with questions like

> "What is the mouse doing?"

> "Where is he taking the strawberry?"

> "How is he trying to hide it?"

As children become more familiar with certain books, invite them to tell you about the story and share story details. Support children at this level by asking questions such as

> "Why did the mouse want to hide the strawberry?"

> "What would happen if the bear found it?"

> "What else could the mouse have done?"

While reading a familiar book for the third or fourth time, stop the story halfway through and ask older preschoolers to make predictions about what they would do next if they were in the story.

When using high-quality children's books in your classroom, remember that each child absorbs information through many different modalities (Rumenapp, Morales, & Lykouretzos 2018). Incorporating gestures, props, and an animated reading voice all help to keep children engaged in a storytelling experience. It is also important to keep in mind that children with auditory or visual processing delays might require more time to process what they hear and see (Brillante 2017). They need repetition to incorporate new information into both short- and long-term memory (Moreno & Mayer 2007).

To extend and recreate favorite and familiar stories from books, offer bookmaking supplies. These can be made from store-bought journals, blank booklets assembled from construction paper and round-head fasteners, or even recycled copier paper that is stapled or taped together. Interesting materials for book making—such as construction paper, hole punchers, and yarn—should be available in the early learning setting and organized so children can access them easily. As children's familiarity, knowledge, and enjoyment of books and reading grows, invite them to create their own original books. Teacher-made, child-made, and family-made books should all be included in various learning center libraries and valued as highly as any other book in the early learning setting.

Story Baskets

Young children are natural storytellers! You can encourage this skill by assembling story baskets that contain an interesting variety items that are found, store bought, or handmade. Note that these are not collections of materials made or bought to intentionally accompany a specific book, such as felt fruit shapes to go with *The Very Hungry Caterpillar* (by Eric Carle) or letter magnets to go with *Chicka Chicka Boom Boom* (by Bill Martin Jr. and John Archambault, illustrated by Lois Ehlert).

Instead, story baskets are random collections of materials to inspire children to exercise their imaginations and become story engineers.

For example, you might include small handheld toys collected from yard sales, finds from consignment or thrift shops, and leftover pieces from old or unusable board games and puzzles. These materials, which often find their way into the garbage or recycling can, are unique and interesting for children. They can spark a conversation or an idea that can lead to a made-up silly story told orally or through emergent writing. Other ideas for story basket items include

> **Natural items:** crystals, stones, pine cones, seashells, acorns, small tree cookies, small unbreakable bottles of sand

> **Recycled materials:** bottle caps, straws, cardboard tubes

> **Store-bought objects:** counting bears, finger puppets, wooden cubes, dollhouse figures, handheld vehicles

Begin with five to 10 objects per story basket; as children become familiar with engaging with the story baskets, you might add one or two more objects. Choose items that represent real and make-believe objects (e.g., a toy depicting a realistic pig as well as a toy depicting a clothed pig). Consider the size of the materials if children are likely to put objects in their mouths. Ideally, the items should be made of different materials and textures, such as wood, plastic, and fabric. Place the story baskets in the literacy center where they are easily accessible to the children. Rotate the objects in the baskets to coordinate with current units of study or children's interests.

As children explore the objects, support their discoveries with thoughtful comments and questions like the following:

> "What are you looking at? Where have you seen a bunny before?" (Identify objects)

> "This bunny's white fur is so soft. And look at its fluffy tail!" (Describe an object's characteristics)

> "I'm going to make up a story about this bunny finding a giant orange carrot." (Self-talk)

If you and the children create an oral story together, ask the children for suggestions on which materials from the story basket to incorporate next. You might also invite children to retell a story you have created using the same materials. Crafting a story using story basket materials is a concrete way to introduce story elements, such as character, plot, and sequence. Encourage children to think of roles that are familiar to them (e.g., teacher, student, hero, mother, father, pet, friend). Over time, children will become more familiar with the activity but may still require adult support when adding and extending details. Ask children to describe what they want to happen in their story and help them develop the language to support their ideas. Older

1. Introduce the story basket and invite each child to choose an item.

2. To model how the story basket works, choose your own item and begin the story with a short statement related to that item: "Once upon a time, there was a shiny red car."

3. Ask each child to add to the story using their prop or "character." Write down *exactly* what each child says.

4. After each child has a turn, read aloud (with animation and interest) what the children have composed so far, holding up each prop as it makes an appearance in the story.

5. Once finished reading the story, ask the children to add more details. For example, "Zanele added this part of the story about the dog going for a walk. What words can we add to describe the dog?" Include the details to the written story in another color to encourage reflecting and editing as part of the creative process.

preschoolers may be able to create their stories independently by combining many materials in the basket or carefully selecting items that go together. As a child tells their story, ask them to explain their choices ("That's so funny! Why did the bunny ride the bus?" or "What would happen if the bunny bought an apple instead of a carrot?").

Conclusion

The materials and activities outlined in this chapter provide creative and interesting ways of incorporating language and literacy in children's play. They offer opportunities for both teacher-guided activities and children's independent play. Language and literacy learning and development are supported through a combination of interactions, conversations, and children's self-directed play.

TECH TIPS

- Place an old keyboard in the writing center for children to find letters.

- Use word-processing software to explore different fonts and styles of letters.

- Record children acting out a story or rhyme while they read a book aloud.

- Use a metronome to keep the beat while reciting rhymes.

- Use your phone or a pocket-size video recorder to capture (and replay) children engaged in storytelling using story basket items.

Suggested Play Materials

Geometry, Shapes, and Spatial Sense

- Blocks and other building toys in a variety of sizes, shapes, and materials (e.g., bristle blocks, DUPLO blocks, linking cubes)
- Craft materials for constructing 2-D shapes (e.g., chenille stems, craft sticks, straws) and 3-D shapes (e.g., clay, hydrophobic sand, playdough)
- Foam attribute shapes
- Geoboards and rubber bands
- Manipulatives in a variety of sizes, shapes, and materials (e.g., Magna-Tiles, parquetry blocks)
- Puzzles with 10–40 pieces composed of and/or depicting geometric shapes
- Recyclable materials in 3-D shapes and of various sizes (e.g., bottle caps, cardboard boxes and tubes, packing foam)
- Shape stencils

Sorting, Comparing, and Patterning

- Beads of varying colors, shapes, and sizes and materials to string them on (e.g., chenille stems, shoelaces, wire, yarn)
- Collections of objects and natural items of varying colors, shapes, and/or characteristics (e.g., bottle caps, counting bears, gems, linking cubes, pom-poms, sea glass, stones)
- Musical instruments with distinguishable sounds (e.g., bells, maracas, tambourines)
- Pattern cards

Measurement

- Balance scales and items to weigh
- Measuring cups and spoons with materials to measure (e.g., birdseed, sand, water)
- Nonstandard measuring tools (e.g., counting links, linking cubes, yarn)
- Standard measuring tools (e.g., height charts, measuring tapes, rulers, thermometers)

Number Sense and Counting

- Abacuses
- Coins from other countries
- Dice with numerals, dots, or algebraic symbols (-, +, =) on their faces
- Dominoes
- Five and ten frames and collections of objects (e.g., flower petals, mini erasers, squash seeds)
- Number cards and collections of objects (e.g., corks, nuts and bolts, river stones)
- Numerals in varying materials that can be manipulated (e.g., felt, magnets)
- Peg boards with numerals printed on them and holes that match the quantity
- Playing cards
- Toy objects or real, nonfunctioning objects that feature numerals (e.g., cash registers, computer keyboards, telephones)

CHAPTER 6

Play Materials That Teach Me Mathematical Concepts

It is important for preschoolers to have experiences with play materials for the specific purpose of math learning. Intentional teachers help children understand that math has uses in their everyday world. For example, asking children to identify and name the shape of a block supports their math content knowledge. Asking them where else they see that same shape in their environment helps them see that math is all around them.

Play materials that can be used to teach specific mathematical concepts are wide ranging. They can include items from nature (e.g., pine cones, seashells), familiar household objects (buttons, clothespins), and materials designed specifically for math learning (e.g., peg boards, tangrams). Having a vast selection of math play materials enables children to explore spatial relationships; gain exposure to numbers, shapes, and attributes; develop an early understanding of operations; and use math as part of their everyday life.

Interesting materials combined with scaffolding and modeling strategies from you, the teacher, help children build understanding and develop foundational skills they will need to apply to more complicated math concepts later. For example, before preschool-age children can subitize—or see a small number of objects and determine how many objects there are without counting them—they need to practice counting and be exposed to language that represents quantity. Likewise, children in this age group begin to explore matching and sorting objects based on one attribute or characteristic (e.g., color, shape, size) before they are ready to sort objects by two or more attributes (Hynes-Berry & Grandau 2019). As mentioned previously, the list of suggested play materials is not comprehensive, but many of the highlighted suggestions are open ended and allow teachers and children to use them in ways that meet the children's needs best. Consider linking cubes: while younger preschoolers might use linking cubes by simply connecting them to create a tower, older preschoolers may use the same play material as the basis for more complex math experiences, such as creating patterns, measuring the length of an object, or graphing data.

Parquetry Blocks

There is a vast assortment of math manipulatives available for children. One great option for preschoolers is parquetry blocks, also known as pattern blocks, which are designed to help young children see how shapes can be decomposed (taken apart) and composed (put together) into other shapes. The variety of shapes, colors, and sizes of these blocks appeal to young children as they begin to see how shapes fit into the space around them and in relation to each other. Store parquetry blocks in a sturdy bin close to a table. If there is no table available, provide large trays that children can use as smooth work surfaces.

When preschoolers are first introduced to parquetry blocks, they may match two of the same shape together. They might recognize or even say that the two blocks are the same but may not yet be able to answer why. To encourage children's vocabulary, incorporate specific mathematical language—including shape names (e.g., *triangle, square, hexagon, rhombus*) and the geometric attributes of shapes (e.g., *vertices, sides, angles*)—during your conversations and interactions with children while they engage with the play material. As children explore the attributes of each individual piece and begin to understand what makes a shape a shape, offer comments and ask questions like the following to help extend children's thinking about the play material's attributes and possibilities:

❭ "Triangles have three points."

❭ "What's this shape called?"

❭ "How can we make this shape using some of the other shapes?"

❭ "The orange shape has four sides."

> "How many sides does this square have?"

> "What's the same (different) about this rhombus and this square?"

Parquetry blocks can be introduced alone or with other materials that support and extend their use, such as pattern cards or mirrors. Pattern cards feature a printed sequential design template for placing the shapes on. Begin with templates that are in full color, ensuring that the colors on the template match the colors of your set of parquetry blocks. Once children have mastered this template version, you might provide pattern cards that feature only the shape outlines and no colors. This encourages children to see the way the shapes work together and can be arranged to create larger patterns. To extend learning further, take away the templates, invite children to design their own patterns, and ask questions like the following:

> "What kind of organizer could you design for sorting these shapes so that all the squares are together, all the triangles are together, and all the rhombuses are together?"

> "What kind of pattern card could you make for your friend to use?"

> "What could you create using this set of shapes?"

Mirrors are another creative companion material for children to use while playing with parquetry blocks. A child may create a simple design or pattern using the blocks and then hold up a mirror next to it to see how the design changes when they view it through the mirror. Concepts like symmetry, balance, and reflection can be introduced and explored when mirrors are added—not to mention the visual interest they provide to keep the children focused and engaged!

Collections of Objects

Collections of objects with a rich variety of colors, shapes, sizes, and textures make great play materials for inspiring sorting, comparing, and patterning. Including materials in your early learning setting that are new and exciting for children is important to engaging their interest and inspiring new kinds of play; however, it is vital to also provide materials with which children are already familiar. Having opportunities to engage with familiar materials in hands-on, new, and unique ways supports children's meaning-making, flexible thinking, and problem-solving skills.

A few collections of objects with interesting attributes children can sort, compare, and pattern with include bottle caps (which often have writing or symbols on them, another attribute beyond color or shape), seashells, and feathers. (Note: Remember that smaller objects could potentially be a choking hazard for younger preschoolers. Refer to the "Safety Considerations" section in Chapter 4.)

When first exploring the patterning potential of collections of objects, invite preschoolers to line up items as they wish. After they have had plenty of time to explore and engage with the materials and you have observed their efforts, comment or pose questions based on the child's developmental level and contexts:

> "I see you organized these leaves in a straight line!"

> "There are a few red LEGO bricks in your line. One here in the beginning, another in the middle, and then one all way here at the end. You repeated the red LEGO bricks in your line."

> "How many times do you see a silver bottle cap in this line?"

> "What was the first bead you chose? Next?"

To support children at the earliest stages of understanding patterns, model creating a simple *ab* repeating pattern (e.g., white button, blue button, white button, blue button, white button, blue button). Encourage children to look for and copy patterns in their environment. You might also ask them to try extending a pattern you create or they find, or provide pattern cards with spaces where they may place items. Continue pointing out the repetition and, eventually, children will try and create patterns on their own.

For children who have had repeated exposure to patterning and are ready for higher-level engagement, create a simple pattern and ask them to repeat the same pattern rule using a completely different set of play materials. This is known as *translating patterns*. Spark this and other patterning challenges with questions like the following:

> ❯ "How could you make this same pattern using these blocks instead of bottle caps?"

> ❯ "What's another way we could use these big and small caps to make a pattern?"

> ❯ "Instead of making a line pattern on the table, what would happen if you stacked the caps on top of each other?"

When children's understanding of simple patterns increases, model and point out more complex *aab* or *abc* patterns for children to copy, extend, translate, and—eventually— create. As their pattern work becomes more sophisticated, update the collections of materials you have available for children to create with. You may, for example, choose to gradually include additional sizes, colors, or shapes of the same material to expand on the variety.

At first, having many collections of objects may seem overwhelming. Begin with two or three collections, ensuring there are enough pieces for a few children to play at a time. As children become familiar with the collections, rotate and expand the collections to encourage different types of learning.

Nonstandard Measuring Tools

Before children learn how to use standard measurement tools like measuring tapes and rulers, they need to develop an understanding of what measuring means. Providing nonstandard measuring tools for children to explore and play with deepens young children's understanding of measurement.

Introduce the idea of measurement to your preschoolers by saying things like

> "We're going to line up these linking cubes next to our book so we can see how long it is."

> "Let's put the chain of counting links at the bottom of your tower and stretch it all away to the top and see where it stops!"

> "Show me the bottom and the top of your Magna-Tiles building."

> "Where is the beginning of this piece of yarn? How about the end?"

To encourage children's exploration of nonstandard measuring tools, place linking cubes and yarn near other small play materials and objects, such as baby dolls or flower stems, or write prompt questions on index cards nearby (e.g., *How many counting links long is your foot?*). Once children are comfortable measuring smaller objects, suggest larger items, such as furniture, an area rug, or a block structure. Ask children for suggestions of things they would like to measure for you to incorporate in the setting.

Provide a basket of yarn pieces cut into different sizes near the book *Just How Long Can a Long String Be?!* (by Keith Baker) so children see that measurements can be compared. After they have developed an understanding of the concept, invite them to compare the lengths of objects, introducing vocabulary such as *longer, taller, shorter, wider,* and *narrower.*

Ask interested children, "How can we create a poster that shows how tall your block building is compared to your friends?" To extend thinking, challenge children to design a building that has the same measurements as another object. Listen to their ideas, and help them try out their solutions to the problems you pose.

Trees, plants, or the children themselves can be measured with nonstandard measuring tools throughout the year and tracked on a poster board to show the differences in height over time. For example, if using yarn, each length of yarn that is used to measure can be added to the poster and labeled to create a bar graph.

Conclusion

Math is present in nearly every part of your early learning setting, from the shapes and patterns on a ball to the beat of a favorite song. The play materials that you choose can focus explicitly on math concepts, such as those that feature numbers and shapes, but through your interactions with children and the questions you ask them, you can mathematize almost any material. Providing open-ended play materials and engaging in thoughtful, intentional activities that encourage math reasoning are important parts of math learning in early childhood.

TECH TIPS

- Download a free random number generator app. Encourage children to create a collection with the specific number of objects the generator has assigned them. All of the objects in their collection should have at least one shared attribute.

- Invite children to use the class digital camera (or an old smartphone that is no longer connected to a service plan) to take photos of shapes they find in their environment.

- Encourage children to use cameras to record videos of themselves creating simple movement patterns with their bodies (e.g., jump, clap, jump, clap, jump, clap).

- Dip small, inexpensive windup toys or robotic creatures (like HEXBUG nanos) in ink or paint. Set them on a piece of paper to walk on. Children can measure the distance the toys travel using yarn or linking cubes.

- Take photos of children's block structures from different perspectives (e.g., top, sides, front, back). Encourage them to recreate their structure from one of the perspectives to support their spatial awareness skills.

Suggested Play Materials

Asking Questions and Formulating Plans

- Blueprints and floor plans of buildings and structures
- Clipboards and carpenter pencils
- Photos of neighborhood buildings
- Rulers and T-squares

Construction

- Blocks in a variety of sizes, shapes, and materials (e.g., cardboard blocks, DUPLO blocks, foam blocks, hollow blocks, KEVA planks, LEGO bricks, unit blocks, wooden cubes)
- Home improvement materials and household objects (e.g., carpet and flooring samples, clothespins, contact paper, wire)
- Natural materials (e.g., pine cones, sticks, stones, tree cookies)
- Playdough and clay
- Ramp-building materials (e.g., cove molding, plastic tubing, pool noodles, PVC pipes, vinyl downspout extensions)
- Recyclable materials (e.g., cardboard boxes and tubes, craft sticks, disposable plates and cups, plastic bottles, straws)

Handling Real Tools

- Carabiners and ropes
- C-clamps and spring clamps
- Hammers and nails
- Hand drills
- Hex keys and hex socket screws
- Levels
- Low-temp glue guns
- Pliers
- Safety goggles and gloves
- Sandpaper with different grits
- Scissors
- Screwdrivers and screws of varying lengths and gauges
- Small saws with handles
- Wrenches and bolts

CHAPTER 7

Play Materials That Encourage Me to Build and Engineer

Young children are increasingly being offered opportunities to engage in the engineering and design process; in fact, recent revisions to various state standards explicitly include references to the provision of these opportunities (see AR DDCECE & ARHSSCO 2016; MA DESE 2016; NYS ED 2019). Some teachers are unsure what play materials are appropriate to support emerging 3- to 5-year-old engineers, but building and engineering materials are all around. Some, like unit blocks and playdough, are already commonly found in preschool settings. Others might be easy to access but are less obvious as play materials—rocks and sticks collected from the playground, empty food boxes, or even vinyl downspout extensions leftover from a home improvement project. Despite their seeming disparity, all of these materials help children develop and strengthen skills that real-world engineers need, including engaging in critical, flexible, and creative thinking to problem solve; organizing, planning, and executing tasks; and working within project constraints and requirements (Heroman 2017).

Looking at play materials through this lens opens the door to many possibilities for how you can present these materials and how children can engage with them in the early learning setting. Children can discover new approaches to interacting with objects, test theories, evaluate results, and examine possible solutions. Relationships between different play materials can be explored as children's attempts at construction are successful (or not). Children can evaluate what is working and what is not and seek feedback from peers and adults to come up with solutions. As young children practice seeing and considering play materials and their environment from an engineer's perspective, they begin to understand how they can interact with and have a role in designing the world around them.

Unit Blocks

"Block play is essential for every child's creative, social-emotional, cognitive, and physical development" (Hansel 2016, 3). For this reason, unit blocks are a standard in most early learning settings. Regardless of the manufacturer or the material from which they are made, unit blocks adhere to a standardized set of measurements. They come in a variety of shapes and sizes and encourage children to experiment with structure and stability, build on their reasoning and critical thinking skills, develop an understanding of spatial awareness, and solve problems. While playing with unit blocks, children also practice skills that reinforce their imagination, understanding of geometric concepts, and ability to think abstractly.

Three-year-olds may take many blocks from the shelves, create piles, or spread them around the floor. This is the first step in developing awareness of the space around them and building their visual–spatial thinking skills (Hansel 2016). As preschoolers begin to understand the properties of the unit blocks, they take the first steps of exploring engineering. Provide children with vocabulary to identify various features of the blocks (e.g., *curve, point, straight, long, short, hard*), and model how blocks can be stacked or arranged using self-talk ("I'm stacking a circle curve on top of a quad unit").

NOW TRY THIS! Making the Most of Unit Blocks in the Block Center

- Organize unit blocks on low, open shelves, arranged by similar type and moving from smallest to largest.

- Research the actual names of the unit blocks (e.g., *column, gothic arch, pillar, small buttress, unit*) and use this high-level vocabulary in your conversations with children.

- Store accessory materials, such as street signs, small buildings, vehicles, and people and animal figures, in labeled containers.

- To inspire more detailed or concrete block play, tape photos of neighborhood buildings to blocks and provide carpet and flooring samples for children to incorporate in their structures.

Observe as children begin to stack blocks vertically, name the structures they have built, or ask for help to create specific structures. Help children describe their efforts by introducing architectural vocabulary (e.g., *eave, roof, turret*) and prompting them to explain their work and ideas ("Have you seen this type of building before? Where?"). As children encounter structural challenges, encourage them to engage in the engineering design process by asking questions that require them to articulate their thinking ("Why do you think your structure keeps falling?"). Children will continue to expand their understanding of stability and balance, moving on to concepts as abstract as gravity and displacement. When children grow confident in their building skills, ask them to hypothesize what would happen if they added more unit blocks to the top of their structure or evaluate what block shapes work best to achieve their goals.

In addition to unit blocks and other construction play materials, provide children with planning and reference resources, such as blueprints and floor plans, as well as materials for sketching out their ideas before they start building. Introduce the design process by inviting them to sketch out their plans, build, and then change their structure to improve it. Once a structure is complete, encourage children to create or use building accessories (e.g., cars for the garage, animals for the zoo, steering wheels for the car) to make their structures come to

life. Ask children questions that encourage them to share their experiences with others ("What kind of book could you create to explain your design process?"). Scaffold this sharing of ideas by guiding them to take step-by-step photos of their structures as they work to complete them.

Ramp-Building Materials

When children build and use ramps or marble runs, they are engaging in the science and engineering processes of exploring force and motion, planning and carrying out investigations, learning cause and effect, and analyzing and interpreting results—all skills that serve them as they continue on to future schooling and success (DeVries & Sales 2010). Children often begin their exploration of ramps by leaning a block against a shelf and rolling a car or ball down the slope. To encourage this exploration, add other novel play materials that can be cut, combined, or otherwise manipulated to create more sophisticated and interesting ramps, such as cove molding, plastic tubing, cardboard tubes, pool noodles (cut lengthwise), PVC pipes, and vinyl downspout extensions. For easy access and cleanup, store ramp-building materials in an umbrella stand.

If some children aren't naturally drawn to playing with ramps, you might introduce them by giving children small (12- to 18-inch) sections of one or two of the previously mentioned ramp-building materials and a golf or Ping-Pong ball and asking if they can think of a way to move the ball without touching it. As children become more familiar with ramps, extend their experiences by encouraging them to adjust the ramp by leaning it against objects with varying heights or to use different types of vehicles or balls. Invite children to describe their actions; listen as they explain their efforts; and introduce vocabulary such as *angle, tilt, higher*, and *lower*. Ask children to comment on the speed of the rolling object as they adjust the ramp's angle. Textures—including sand paper, felt, corrugated cardboard, and double-sided contact paper—can also be added to the surface of the incline to create friction, increase the challenge, and provide opportunities for exploring cause and effect.

Support children in creating a more complex course for the ball or car to travel through, using scientific terminology in your interactions:

> "Your ramp has a steep angle, and it made the ball have more *energy* because it went faster."

> "The car has no *velocity* because it is not moving up the ramp."

> "When you pushed the ball, it moved. Your hand put *force* on it."

Ramps are also opportunities for children to exercise their working memory as they test out theories and ideas. The more children use them, the more ways they will be able to discover new solutions, strategize, and achieve their design goals. Pay attention to the comments children make, and help them to identify the exact point where their ramp setup is not working. Guide them to experiment and problem solve.

Disposable Cups

Most likely, the children you teach are familiar with disposable cups from their everyday life, but have they ever built with them? Disposable cups offer children opportunities to create structures that challenge their problem-solving skills and help them develop spatial awareness. Using cups as building materials also asks children to question and unlearn what they know about this familiar object and adjust their views. They are inspired to rethink the possibilities and potential of all kinds of everyday items. After all, if disposable cups

aren't just for drinking, what else might they be used for? Because disposable cups are lightweight, teachers may feel more comfortable encouraging children to build higher structures with them as compared to other construction materials (e.g., blocks) without fear of injury.

Stack cups on a shelf or in a bin for easy access and use. If there are cups available in multiple sizes, you might arrange them from smallest to largest. Begin by introducing one size of cup. As children become more familiar with using them, add different sizes. Encourage children to compare characteristics and create structures using the different-size disposable cups (e.g., a pyramid made using one level of nine-ounce cups and one level of six-ounce cups, a tower of cups stacked from largest to smallest or the reverse). Disposable cups can also be combined with other recyclable materials (e.g., cardboard boxes, Styrofoam, paper plates) or with different types of blocks (e.g., cardboard blocks, foam blocks, unit blocks) to encourage children's ability to engineer and design.

Extend children's use of disposable cups by imitating their actions and using self-talk to describe what you are doing ("I'm taking a big red cup and putting it on the floor. Now I'm taking a paper plate and putting it on top of the cup. I hope it doesn't fall"). To scaffold children's learning, ask questions and make comments like the following:

> "How many cups did you use?"

> "Tell me about the size of the cups."

> "I wonder what would happen if I turned this cup upside down."

> "How has your tower changed since you started with the first cup at the bottom?"

> "What is different about building with blocks compared to building with cups? What do you like about building with cups?"

Children might also use disposable cups to create games with an element of engineering. Encourage this kind of play by challenging them to design components for different parts of gameplay (e.g., catching balls at the end of a ramp, rapidly stacking up and breaking down cup towers, lining them up as targets).

Conclusion

The play materials explored in this chapter provide easy entry points for teachers looking to encourage building and engineering in their early learning settings. Many of the materials are easily accessible or already in your learning setting or home and are destined for the garbage or recycling bin as you spring clean. Rethinking how these materials can be used opens the door for children to explore and develop their building and engineering skills. Children's creativity and ingenuity should be valued and supported while they engage with these play materials. The key is to consistently encourage them to plan their design; test their creation; and try, try, try again!

TECH TIPS

- Go online with children to look up photos, blueprints, or floor plans of structures similar to those they want to build.

- Provide digital cameras for children to take photos to document their building progress and completed efforts.

- Encourage children to search online for maps of familiar places (e.g., the local museum or zoo, the neighborhood around the program) and recreate them using the play materials in the setting.

- Invite children to create small-scale obstacle courses for them to navigate using tablet-controlled robots (like Sphero mini robot balls).

- Watch videos of Rube Goldberg machines (complicated machines designed to do simple tasks), and ask children to describe the steps they observe. Help children to design and, if possible, construct their own.

Suggested Play Materials

Chemistry

- Clear squeeze bottles
- Food coloring
- Liquid substances (e.g., baby oil, corn syrup, vegetable oil, white vinegar)
- Plastic test tubes
- Powder substances (e.g., baking soda, cornstarch, flour, salt, sugar)

Creative Problem Solving

- Fasteners (e.g., binder clips, duct tape, rubber bands)
- Home improvement materials (e.g., PVC pipes, wooden dowels)
- Magnets
- Materials for embroidering or sewing (e.g., embroidery hoops, fabric scraps, plastic sewing needles, sewing floss)
- Recyclable materials (e.g., cardboard boxes and tubes, plastic bottles, straws)
- Rope
- Simple machines (e.g., levers, pulleys, wedges)
- Tools (e.g., clamps, hammers and nails, hand drills, low-temp glue guns, pliers, screwdrivers and screws)

Electronics

- Batteries
- Broken or outdated electronics and toys (e.g., computer keyboards, cordless phones, battery-operated or windup toys)
- Circuit-building and coding kits
- Electrical tape
- Hobby motors
- Homemade circuit blocks
- String lights

CHAPTER 8

Play Materials That Inspire Scientific Inquiry and Innovation

Young children are naturally inquisitive. The novelty of everything they come across provides them with plenty of opportunities to wonder how things work as they explore the world around them. Early childhood educators actively encourage this curiosity and support children as they seek inventive, hands-on ways to find answers to their questions and solutions to the problems they encounter. These challenges can be as simple as figuring out how to open a watercolor set that dry paint has crusted shut or as complex as coming up with a way to retrieve a toy car stuck underneath a piece of furniture that is too heavy to move.

Play materials in this category should be open ended, unusual, and provided in response to children's interests and real problem-solving needs in their environment. Wonder aloud as children explore, interact, and create with the materials. When you begin a sentence with "I wonder," you invite children to join you in the question and encourage them to ask their own *how* and *why* questions. The children become authentic thought partners as you engage them in shared curiosity.

Inviting children to explain why something occurred, or what could be done differently next time, supports children's developing inquiry skills (Ramanathan, Carter, & Wenner 2021). Consider this series of questions to a child using a small hobby motor:

> "What is your plan to power the motor?"

> "Why did you choose the double-A battery to turn the motor on?"

> "What would happen if you used a C battery instead of a double-A battery?"

Resist the urge to make things easier for children by providing them with answers or resolving challenges for them before they have had the opportunity to try for themselves. Teachers often solve simple problems for children without intending to. You may casually open the playdough container, fix a leaning block tower, or button up a doll's dress. Instead of solving these problems for children, use them as opportunities for children to create innovative solutions to these everyday challenges.

Liquid and Powder Substances

Ignite children's interest in scientific learning and spark curiosity by offering opportunities for basic chemistry. Children can mix safe liquids and powders to explore reactions. Provide children with clear squeeze bottles similar to those from a baking or beauty supply store. These bottles are made from lightweight plastic and can be squeezed easily. They are also transparent, allowing children to see inside and decide which substances they want to mix. Fill the bottles with plain water, water tinted with food coloring, vegetable oil, corn syrup, white vinegar, salt, sugar, baking soda, baby oil, or flour. Plastic test tubes or clear cups are perfect for combining these substances.

After introducing the basic concept of solution mixing, gradually add more substances to your collection so children can explore more combinations and observe different reactions. They will begin to understand that different combinations have different results. Before choosing substances, research any possible unintended combinations to prevent those that produce heat or are toxic. Children need plenty of opportunities to explore, and as they make discoveries, introduce them to science vocabulary ("Your *solution* is thick," "The *reaction* is making bubbles"). Introduce different substances during follow-up small group activities, or let children discover the reactions on their own. (Note: While these substances are nontoxic, ingesting them could potentially still make a child ill. Keep a close eye on this kind of independent play.)

Older preschoolers can plan for the substances they want to combine and develop graphs or logs to categorize and document their results. It is important to give them more freedom to experiment. Invite children to explain why they are making certain predictions, and encourage them to draw connections from previous learning. For example, you might say

> "I noticed that you mixed blue and yellow water before, and it made green. What do you think would happen if you mixed blue and red water?"

> "You made a lot of bubbles when you mixed soap and water. I wonder if there are any other substances that will make bubbles."

When introducing chemistry concepts into your early learning setting, here are some steps you might take:

1. Introduce two familiar substances, like sugar and water, during a small group lesson.

2. Give each child a cup of water and a few packets of sugar, and encourage them to smell and touch each substance.

3. Invite children to combine the substances in a test tube or cup.

4. Place a few spoons, craft sticks, or coffee stirrers on the table to see if children choose to use them. Observe how children stir or shake the solution, and introduce vocabulary words like *swirl*, *agitate*, and *swoosh*.

5. Some children may notice as sugar floats to the bottom of the tube. Ask them to describe what they see ("How are the sugar granules moving through the water?," "What is happening to the sugar?").

6. As children observe the sugar granules, encourage them to mix the solution (either for the first time or again) to see the effect the movement has on the sugar in the tube.

7. Place a bucket nearby to eliminate the need for children to run back and forth to the sink to empty their tubes.

Pulleys

Simple machines like pulleys invite children to experience the ways tools can be used to solve real problems and develop innovative solutions. Pulleys require more initial assistance and guidance from teachers. Before introducing pulleys to the children, familiarize yourself with how pulleys work so you can demonstrate their use to children.

Start by incorporating or identifying their use in the play children are already engaged in. For example, if children wash doll clothes and hang them to dry on a clotheslines pulley, point out the clothesline and comment on how the rope moves as you slide it ("Look how the rope goes around the pulley. It makes it easier to get the clothes from one end to the other"). Ask children to make observations about how the rope is moving around the pulley and encourage them to identify the moving parts. After children have experimented and become familiar with the clothesline pulley, set up a challenge for the children by taking the clothesline apart. As needed, guide them in reassembling the clothesline by looping the rope around the pulley and observing how the wheel spins.

You might also suggest a few learning centers that could use a pulley system:

> A bucket and pulley system in the block center to lift blocks onto tall structures

> A PVC pipe scaffolding around the sensory table with a pulley attached to the top to fill and empty buckets of water

> A pulley system in the art center to lift and gently pour cups of paint onto canvases

As children become more familiar with how pulleys work, they can think of and develop their own methods for moving things around. Ask children, "How can we make this job easier?" and be prepared for an avalanche of ideas! Engage children in conversations, asking them about their plans for the pulley and how they want to use it. If children seem to struggle, suggest ways to modify their idea and reassure them that this is all a part of the design process. This is the very definition of innovation.

For children who need more of a challenge, offer double-wheel pulleys or even different types of rope or cording. Don't be discouraged if children aren't engaging with the pulleys right away. Unfamiliar materials take more time, and children may need more modeling and guidance.

Broken or Outdated Electronics and Toys

Exploring how things work is at the heart of promoting inquiry and innovation in young learners. Investigating the inner workings of broken or outdated electronics and toys can lead to fascinating lines of inquiry led by the children. Place old electronics—such as computer keyboards, cordless phones, digital alarm clocks, and speakers—in your science learning center or makerspace. Include screwdrivers, hammers, pliers, and clamps so that children have the tools needed to engage in breaking down their parts.

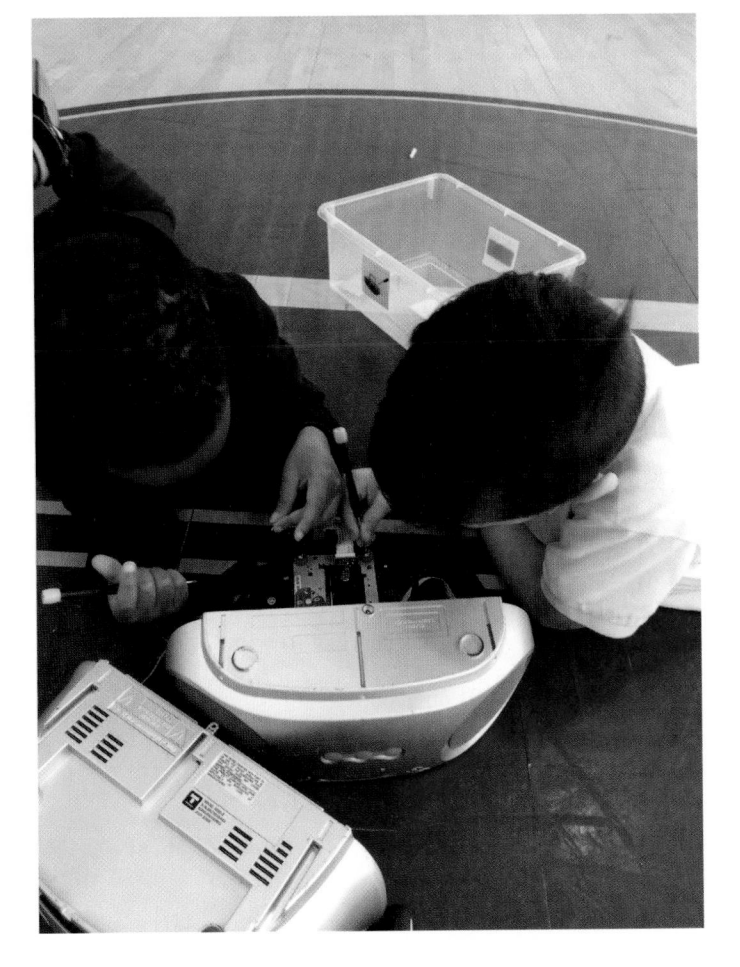

Introduce and reinforce safety procedures for engaging with the materials, such as wearing child-size safety gloves and glasses while using tools. Work with the children to develop a clear list of rules using both written and rebus language (that is, a combination of symbols and pictures). Post the rules nearby and refer to them frequently. Having these procedures in place may help to alleviate some of the anxiety about using real tools in the early learning setting.

If young children are unsure of how to begin taking apart electronics, work side by side with them, offering encouragement and demonstrating how to use the tools. For children who are still working on their fine motor skills, you might help prevent frustration by lightly holding the tip of the screwdriver while the child turns it to remove screws.

Once children gain more experience taking apart electronics, ask them to predict what they think may be inside. Children may be surprised and excited by the things they find inside these old machines. You may even find yourself amazed at how these simple electronics are more complex than expected. Encourage this sense of wonder and invite children to ask their own questions about how objects in their environment work. Children can catalog the parts they find and make connections between them. Engage in conversations with the children to see if they have ideas on how to reuse and repurpose some of the pieces they find.

Not all children will be able to fully realize their ideas independently, and they may not succeed on their first, second, or even third attempts. Therefore, teachers may need to guide and make recommendations to children to help them achieve their goals. Remember, let children take the lead; your suggestions should be a support, not a solution. If children experience frustration, reassure them that it is okay to make mistakes and that through discovering what does not work, they can discover what does.

Conclusion

At first, you may find it challenging to continue to add to the list of specific and concrete play materials that encourage inquiry and innovation. When considering what play materials support children in learning and developing these skills, ask yourself if the material

> Encourages children to wonder

> Is open ended

> Provides opportunities for children to solve their own problems

Whatever play materials you choose, consider the developmental levels and abilities of the children in your setting and how the children engage in inquiry-based learning and discovery. The goal should always be to challenge children but not frustrate them.

Suggested Play Materials

Animals and Where They Live

- Animal footprint stamps and ink pads
- Craft and recyclable materials for replicating animal habitats (e.g., cardboard boxes and cylinders, newspapers, playdough, yarn)
- Live animals in observable habitats (e.g., ant or earthworm farms, fish aquariums, hermit crab terrariums)
- Natural materials (e.g., cattails, dried grass, palm fronds, pine cones, tree bark)
- Real animal coverings and homes (e.g., bird feathers, bird nests, honeycombs, sheep wool, snail shells)
- Small, realistically proportioned animal figures (e.g., fish, insects, mammals)

Plants and How They Grow

- Gardening tools (e.g., small pots, soil, watering cans)
- Live plants and plant terrariums
- Magnifying glasses
- Masking tape bracelets for collecting natural materials
- Matching or sequencing games about the life cycle of plants
- Microscopes
- Posters and other display materials with realistic representations of plants
- Seeds for plants, flowers, and vegetables

Weather and Its Effects

- Containers for collecting and tools for measuring rain or snow (e.g., linking cubes, rulers)
- Dress-up clothing and doll clothing for various types of weather (e.g., raincoats, snow boots, sunglasses)
- Fans (e.g., battery-operated mini fans, hand fans)
- Hanging wind chimes and streamers
- Items that reflect and refract light (e.g., CDs, crystals, prisms, silver paper)
- Kites
- Weather charts

CHAPTER 9

Play Materials That Help Me Understand Nature

Learning about nature extends beyond the names of animals and the sounds they make. Positive experiences in nature help young children develop an appreciation and respect for the natural world. Moreover, instilling children with a sense of environmental responsibility and an understanding of the interdependence among people, animals, plants, and the planet we all share is more important than ever. Participating in both structured and unstructured hands-on experiences with nature and natural materials from an early age allows young children to engage in more complex investigations and knowledge building as they get older (Meier & Sisk-Hilton 2017). This chapter highlights play materials that encourage children to discover how nature relates to their everyday experiences.

Craft, Recyclable, and Natural Materials for Replicating Animal Habitats

Many preschoolers love animals, and that interest serves as a great entry point into learning all kinds of information about living creatures, including where they live, or their habitats. Exploring habitats helps children appreciate nature as a place where animals find food, water, and shelter.

A fun way young children can make meaning of the concept of animal habitats is by using play materials to recreate them, from nests to burrows to coral reefs. All manner of play materials can be used in children's habitat-building efforts, but a good starting point is a wide range of craft, recyclable, and natural materials. For creating miniature replicas indoors, this could include cardboard cylinders, dried grass, sand, and yarn as well as animal figures. Children's imaginations and creative thinking skills are fully engaged as they decide which materials best represent the various components of an animal's habitat: chenille stems as cacti, playdough as stalactites, real acorns as a chipmunk's winter food hoard—the possibilities are endless! In more spacious areas, such as outdoors, children can construct large-scale habitat structures using materials like cardboard boxes, palm fronds, and old rubber tires. For habitats both small and large, provide materials that also encourage children to practice skills like weaving, tying, and balancing. With your guidance, children develop an understanding of "home" that extends beyond their own house. Examining how people and animals build and care for their homes opens up discussions about caring for the earth and viewing it as a much larger home, one we share with all living things.

Depending on where children's interests lie, they might choose to focus on creating habitats for animals that are native to where they live or exploring animals and habitats that they are completely unfamiliar with. Regardless of which direction children choose, help them relate animal habitats and behaviors to their own environments and experiences. Here are a few ideas for the kinds of comparisons you might bring to children's attention:

> When discussing anthills, show a photo or video of the inside of one or, if possible, bring in an ant farm and compare it to your early learning setting ("The series of tunnels that the ants excavate look like the hallways in our school! It's how the ants get from place to place, like us").

> While observing an animal's behaviors and expressions in person, in print materials, or on video, invite children to connect what they see to their own behaviors and emotions ("The lion in this photo has his mouth wide open and his eyes are closed. I've seen you do that when you wake up from rest time. I wonder how he's feeling").

> If children notice a bird or squirrel nest inside a tree trunk, relate it to their bed at home ("Squirrels use leaves and moss to create nests that keep them warm and dry while they sleep. What sort of things keep you warm and comfortable while you sleep?").

Gardening Tools and Seeds

Watching a small seed sprout from the earth is a powerful experience for a young child. Maintaining a class garden gives children the opportunity to not only observe this event but also participate in making it happen. When introducing the concept of how plants, flowers, and vegetables grow, invite children to share their ideas about what seeds need to grow; follow their lead as you discuss soil, sunlight, and water; and ask guiding questions that will provoke children to think more deeply or engage in exploratory play ("Why does the seed need to be placed in soil?," "I wonder what would happen if we put this small potted plant in the closet instead of out in the sun"). Provide tools like spades, watering cans, and work gloves and demonstrate their use in caring for plants.

Begin your garden with something relatively easy to grow that has a shorter growing season, such as bush beans or snow peas (Eartheasy, n.d.). Carrot tops are another great low-maintenance option; the leaves of the carrot top sprout quickly and eventually produce flowers. Once children are more practiced at caring for plants, you can expand to seeds that children are more familiar with and readily have on hand, such as orange seeds leftover from lunch. Before planting anything, make sure your selections are not harmful to the children you teach. The National Capital Poison Center (www.poison.org/articles/plant) provides a robust list of poisonous and nonpoisonous plants.

Gardening can be a yearlong activity, and your class garden can take many forms. If your early learning program has the room, landscaped areas around the building can be transformed into children's personal gardens. Involve children in clearing out dead leaves and weeds, digging trenches, and preparing and turning over the soil to ready it for a new season of planting and growth. Consider composting leftover food scraps from mealtimes or celebrations (like fall pumpkins) in the garden so that children can observe decomposition in action. Alternately, invest in raised beds that can be built around the children's outdoor play area. Old sandboxes and plastic kiddie pools can also be converted into garden beds.

For early learning settings with less space—or simply to accommodate gardening in the winter—plants like alyssum and winter honeysuckle can be grown in small pots or window planters. Flower bulbs are another good option for indoor growing. Place a bulb in a transparent container filled with rocks. Nestle the bulb on top of the rocks, and add just enough water to reach the bottom of the bulb. This type of container offers new lines of questioning and observation opportunities as the flower bulb grows ("What will we see first, a sprout or the roots? What about next after that?").

Fans

Young children absorb information through their senses, and they learn to recognize the weather by what they see and feel. Wind occurs in all seasons and in all kinds of weather (sunny, rainy, snowy), making it an excellent focus for children's exploration at any time of year. Fans, whether they are simple hand fans or battery-operated mini fans, can be incorporated in the early learning setting so that children can experiment with generating their own "wind" and observing its effects. For example, a child might use a fan to cool off on a hot day or to try moving other objects, such as wind chimes or streamers. Comments and questions from the teacher can spark new avenues of play and curiosity for children ("I wonder why fanning myself makes me feel more comfortable when it's too warm," "Wow! You made such a forceful breeze with that fan that you made the wind chimes jingle. What other things do you think the fan could move?").

Explorations of how wind moves objects can also integrate math learning. For example, children can collect materials of different weights (e.g., cotton balls, leaves, rocks) from the learning environment and attempt to move them with the wind they generate using a fan. They can then create a chart showing which objects moved and which did not. Encourage children to explain their observations and ideas as they explore the power of wind using the fans. Extend children's learning by introducing complex vocabulary that describes different intensities of wind (e.g., *breeze, draft, gale, gust*) and inviting them to experiment with generating different intensities of wind using fans (e.g., waving a hand fan gently, turning a mini fan to its highest setting).

During conversations about wind (either naturally occurring or generated by fans), include some thoughtful questions and comments like the following:

> "What happens to your hair when you hold a fan in front of your face?"

> "Do you see the leaves blowing on the trees? That's the wind moving them. Do you think a fan could make wind strong enough to move all those leaves?"

> "When the wind is blowing on your body, what does it feel like? Does it feel different when you fan yourself?"

Giving children the opportunity to experiment with something that they cannot see, like the wind, helps them to practice their abstract thinking. Scaffold children's understanding by having conversations about how the wind might affect the things they do, using fans as a concrete support ("During what time of year do you think people are most likely to use a fan? Why?," "Can you think of ways the wind changes the things we do?"). This can lead to a deeper discussion of weather and its impact on children's everyday lives.

Conclusion

Children's interactions with nature are diverse (Kahn, Weiss, & Harrington 2018), from exploring how animals live to planting seeds to determining what they will wear that day based on the weather. There are many things to be learned about the way nature impacts us and the way we, in turn, impact nature. Positive experiences with nature at an early age shape children's relationship with the environment. While laying the foundation for understanding the complex systems of nature is important, so is the magic of watching a prism twinkle in the sun or watching snow fall.

TECH TIPS

- Go online and view a live animal cam feed with children to observe animals in their natural or zoo habitats.

- Download photos of animals onto a tablet or another device capable of enlarging or zooming in on photos so children can study the details present in animal coverings (e.g., fur, feathers, scales), flowers, and raindrops.

- Make digital cameras and printers available for taking and printing photos of growing plants to observe and document their changes over time.

- Look up and share time-lapse videos of natural events (e.g., storms forming, birds building nests, spiders weaving a web, squirrels gathering nuts) to further children's understanding of nature's processes.

- Invite children to use a digital thermometer for measuring the temperature outside. Encourage them to track the temperature over a period of one to two weeks and create a graph.

- Download apps such as PictureThis or Rock Identifier onto a tablet for children to use as they identify plants, flowers, and other natural objects.

Summary and Reflection

The play materials highlighted in Part Two are open ended and encourage children to express their interests and unique viewpoints. They offer ways for children to expand their cognitive thinking and problem-solving skills while also honoring their prior experiences and knowledge. Staying mindful of the experiences that children bring to your classroom creates a positive climate of knowledge seeking, discovery, and wonder.

. . . .

Now Ask Yourself This

- What is something significant you've learned about yourself through your personal hobbies?

- How do you feel when someone listens to your ideas and is a true thought partner to you?

- What does the way children engage with play materials tell you about their connection to them?

- Which of the areas of cognitive learning and development discussed in Part Two do you feel most connected to? How does that impact your teaching of that area?

PART THREE

· ·

Social and Emotional Learning and Development

It is important that each of our children see themselves reflected in the books, dolls, and other materials around the room to help nurture their sense of belonging.

—Gera Jacobs and Kathy Crowley, *Reaching Standards and Beyond in Kindergarten: Nurturing Children's Sense of Wonder and Joy in Learning*

Suggested Play Materials

Turn-Taking, Negotiating, and Compromising

- Board and card games that require two or more players (e.g., Candy Land, Chutes and Ladders, Jenga, Hungry Hungry Hippos, KerPlunk, Memory Match, Slapjack, UNO)
- Cooperative playground equipment (e.g., seesaws, tandem tricycles, wagons)
- Fort-building kits
- Heavy or large materials for carrying cooperatively (e.g., Big Waffle Blocks, buckets filled with dirt or water, oversized wooden blocks and planks made for outdoor play)
- Yarn balls to detangle

Recognizing, Labeling, and Acting Out Emotions

- Cards and charts with faces displaying emotions
- Dolls, soft puppets, and stuffed animals
- Figurines with interchangeable faces/emotions
- Mood meters

Managing Feelings, Behaviors, and Sensory Needs

- Emotion and worry stones
- Interactive displays (e.g., classroom helper charts, emotions posters, linear daily schedules)
- Soft, cozy furniture and objects (e.g., area rugs, beanbag chairs, crib mattresses, pillows, weighted blankets)
- Substances that respond to touch (e.g., clay, sand, soil, water)
- Yoga pose cards and mats

Play Materials That Support My Emotional Intelligence, Relationship Building, and Cooperation Skills

Young children learn best when there is joy in learning, but they also need to feel safe and cared for before they are able to learn academic skills (NAEYC 2020, 2022). The social and emotional well-being of preschoolers is largely guided by teacher–child and peer interactions and supported through the learning environment and intentionally selected play materials. We live in a social world, and in order for children to participate in cooperative learning or in learning new and challenging skills, they need to develop self-confidence as well as positive relationships with others (Torres, Domitrovich, & Bierman 2015).

Children who learn to identify and manage their emotions are better prepared for the years to come, both in education and in life (Józsa & Barrett 2018). They are able to understand their feelings and know how and when to appropriately express them. When children are taught strategies to develop this kind of emotional intelligence, they can better engage in learning activities and have more positive relationships with their peers (Tominey et al. 2017). Having an emotional connection to what they are learning also helps children retain information (Shuster 2000).

Isenberg and Jalongo (2018) categorize the social and emotional learning and development of early learning settings into four categories:

> **Climate** can be thought of as the general mood in the early learning setting. In many ways, the climate guides how well children progress in all domains of learning and development.

> **Relationships** refer to dynamics between a child and their peers and between a child and the educator.

> **Space** refers to the organization of the learning environment as well as play materials.

> **Time** considers the daily routine, how children transition between different parts of the day, and the amount of time children engage in different types of learning.

When reflecting on the climate, relationships, space, and time of your early learning setting, consider these questions as preschoolers engage with play materials and when social conflicts arise:

> Is there a "right" or "wrong" way for children to engage with play materials?

> Are children given plenty of opportunities for open-ended exploration and experimenting?

> How do you respond when children's play leads to things like spilled paint or knocked over objects?

> Do children seem interested in engaging with the play materials provided?

> Does the organization of play materials and children's in-progress and finished products (e.g., block constructions, artwork) support the children's independence?

> Is the space crowded, increasing conflicts and aggressive behavior, or is there ample space to engage with play materials without children tripping over one another?

> Is there a lot of fighting over play materials? Are there enough interesting play materials—or multiples of the most popular ones—so children don't argue over the favorite items?

Tips for Welcoming Children and Families

Part of cultivating a positive climate in your early learning setting includes making all children and families feel welcome, honored, and respected. Here are a few ideas to get you started:

- **Create a welcoming entryway area.** Add inviting and personalized touches to the space where families and visitors first enter your early learning setting. This might include a welcome mat, a small table with a notebook where families can sign in and out, decor and wall hangings that reflect the cultures of the children and families you serve, a bulletin board with information, and photos shared by families and caregivers. This sends the message that each family is a welcome and important part of the classroom community.

- **Personalize cubbies.** Encourage children to decorate their cubby space with drawings, photos, or artifacts from home. Incorporating these materials gives teachers conversation starters with children and their families.

- **Find favorites.** Encourage each child to think about their favorite place or favorite play material in the early learning setting. What is it about the space or material that draws them to it? Forming an attachment to places and play materials can help children feel comfortable and safe, an important part of their overall social and emotional well-being.

> How do you respond when there is a conflict between two children about a play material?

> How long are children engaged in self-directed play throughout the day versus being required to engage in whole group, teacher-directed activities? Does the daily routine balance whole group, small group, and independent play? Does the daily routine "breathe," with alternating times of restful activities and high-activity ones?

> What is the overall feeling during transition times (e.g., smooth, stressful, tense)? Are children given notice before transitions happen?

> Are children left with nothing engaging to do or think about for long periods of time?

This chapter highlights play materials that encourage children's social play and relationships with peers and educators as well as recognition and communication of their emotions. When choosing play materials that support emotional intelligence, relationship building, and cooperation in the early learning setting, consider if the material does one or more of the following:

> Helps children identify their own emotions

> Supports the process of young children learning how their actions affect others

> Encourages cooperation and sharing

> Offers developmentally appropriate ways of expressing emotions

> Supports the basic emotional needs of children ages 3 to 5 to feel safe, secure, and cared for

Board and Card Games

The inherently collaborative nature of some play materials nurtures children's development of empathy, compassion, and trust. While children should never be forced to share play materials, encourage them when they show interest in their peers or signs of entering into cooperative play. The play materials you provide to help preschoolers practice turn-taking should have a primary goal of cooperation, as opposed to competition.

Board and card games can be an excellent way to foster turn-taking skills among preschoolers. Games that involve winning and losing are a controversial subject in early childhood. Because of the egocentric nature of 3-, 4-, and 5-year-olds, losing a game can sometimes cause issues. For this reason, the traditional rules of board and card games need not always apply; any game can be modified to support collaboration. When playing Candy Land, for example, instead of having the first person who reaches Candy Castle be the winner, before gameplay begins, you might say something like "Okay, everybody. When the last person makes it to the end of the candy path, we win! Come on, everybody, cheer your friends on!" Encouraging children to think about games this way fosters teamwork, cooperation, and celebration of the group's collective success.

Children can also participate in this reframing of board and card gameplay. When first introducing a board or card game to children, ask them for ideas on how to use them. For example, you might say, "I have playing cards here. Can you think of a game we can play with them?" Children may offer ideas based on their prior experiences seeing family members play card games or on their own experience seeing materials with numbers on them. Incorporate children's ideas into gameplay and, as necessary, revisit and revise the rules of the new game.

With your guidance and support, children will create their own inclusive rules for playing a game. Providing opportunities like this also helps children develop critical thinking and creativity skills, preparing them for future success (Partnership for 21st Century Learning 2019).

Interactive Displays

Well-planned display materials—which often include photos, drawings, and children's work—engage children's curiosity and provide children with a sense of ownership in the early learning setting. For a display to be most effective, it should be interactive, individualized, and relevant to the events in your learning space (Harms, Clifford, & Cryer 2014). Using displays as play materials with children contributes an additional layer of opportunity to extend their understanding of concepts. When considering interactive displays that support children's emotional intelligence, relationships with others, and their role in the early learning setting, think about the following questions:

> Why am I choosing to include this display?

> How does this display support children's sense of belonging in the learning setting?

> What opportunities does this display provide to invite children to explore different ways to communicate their feelings and ideas, with and without words?

> Will all the children have the opportunity to expand their understanding while interacting with this display?

One interactive display that is helpful for preschoolers is a linear schedule, which is a visual and hands-on representation of time. List each part of the day on a large poster board with an arrow that children can move along as each part happens. Alternately, you might also write each part of the daily routine on separate cards. The cards can be clipped with clothespins to a string hung along the wall and flipped over as each part of the day passes. Knowing what is coming next in the day is an important piece of the social and emotional climate of the classroom.

It reduces stress and inconsistency and helps children anticipate transitions, which, in turn, ensures smoother transition times. Any changes to the daily routine can also be noted on this schedule. For example, if there is a special guest visiting or an event happening, (e.g., picture day, a puppet show, a shortened window of self-directed play), a linear schedule lets children know about this change before the day starts.

Another display material you might include in your early learning setting is a classroom helper chart. For a preschooler, *community* is a broad term. It refers to the place they live as well as the people who live and work there. How then, do you support them in developing a sense of connection to their community and make it relevant to the early learning setting? Assigning classroom helper roles and creating a chart to outline these roles is one concrete way to build this connection while also fostering cooperation and teamwork. By taking on a role similar to community workers in their neighborhood, children are shown the importance of responsibility and get to see how their actions affect others. As young children discover firsthand how and why a community works together, it contextualizes the idea that community is not just about identifying different jobs but also about understanding how these individuals work together. When describing the idea of classroom community, use sweeping hand gestures to emphasize

Community Jobs and Classroom Helpers

Classroom helpers have long been a staple in early learning settings. Roles can, of course, vary depending on the community your program serves, but here are just a few ideas for classroom helper jobs:

Classroom Helper Job Title	What the Role Entails
Botanist	Caring for plants
Coach	Encouraging peers to do their best
Electrician	Turning the lights on and off
Meteorologist	Reporting on the weather to the class
Sanitation worker	Making sure learning centers are organized after self-directed play
Street sweeper	Cleaning up around the sand table
Veterinarian	Feeding and helping to care for the class pet

Engaging in conversations helps children better understand how community roles relate to their own lives. For example, you might show children a photo of a garbage truck and say, "This is a garbage truck, and these people are sanitation workers. They help take trash away and clean up messes in the neighborhood." Some prompts to promote deep thinking and discussions might include

- "Tell me about a time when something was really messy."

- "What are some things we do to keep our classroom clean?"

- "How do you feel when your friend helps you clean up?"

In the case of sanitation workers, it also relays how important it is to clean up materials in the early learning setting, just like sanitation workers clean up the neighborhood.

that it is inclusive and whole. You can also encourage group problem solving by asking questions like "Each one of us has a job in our classroom community. What else needs to be taken care of?"

Finally, include interactive displays that help young children communicate what they are feeling and what they need to feel better. In addition to a "How do you feel?" poster with photos of children's faces depicting different emotions, offer alternative ways for children to let you know how they are feeling. If a child cannot yet describe what they are feeling in words, encourage them to connect their emotions to a concrete idea they are already familiar with: color. Consider the phrases we use as adults to describe feelings with color (e.g., feeling blue, green with envy, seeing red, look for the silver lining). Display a poster with a variety of rich colors that evoke certain moods, like the four-square chart called a *mood meter* (Tominey et al. 2017). Children can place their photo or name tag in the color section that best aligns to their feelings. Engage in a conversation with children about how each color makes them feel ("Which color best shows how you're feeling right now?").

When they choose a color, ask why they chose that color. A mood meter poster offers a unique perspective on social and emotional communication and what to do when words fail.

Adding play materials that promote expression of emotions also provides opportunities to expand children's emotional vocabulary. Consider these alternatives:

> Instead of *happy*, you might say *comforted, content, cozy, creative, expressive, inspired*, or *joyful*.

> Instead of *sad*, you might say *disappointed, embarrassed, lonely, melancholy*, or *worried*.

> Instead of *mad*, you might say *angry, confused, frustrated, fuming, furious*, or *misunderstood*.

As children gain more specific vocabulary to label emotions, their ability to more accurately identify their own feelings and the feelings of others improves.

Soft, Cozy Furniture and Objects

Consider your own daily experiences and routines: How do you feel when you relax on a couch with soft cushions or wrap a soft blanket around yourself while reading a book or watching TV? How does it affect your mood and productivity when you feel uncomfortable? The relief of coming home, taking off your shoes, and sinking onto the couch is an experience that needs to be considered as vital for young children as well.

Often, young children are in group settings for upward of 10 to 12 hours per day. Creating a space with play materials and furnishings that offer a private, comfortable retreat for children who need quiet or less stimulation is crucial for their well-being. A cozy area where children may lie down, hold a soft toy, or stroke a fuzzy blanket can help a child calm down enough to gain control over their emotions. Three- to 5-year-olds are concrete learners, and the idea of feeling comfortable and safe is a somewhat abstract concept. Play materials help them connect with the concept on a sensory level and nurtures their understanding of how these feelings can be brought into the early learning setting.

When deciding which materials are defined as *cozy*, consider how the material responds to touch. Materials like pillows, blankets, and stuffed or beanbag animals move and change form. Fabric and soft cushions, for example, mold to children's bodies, providing a feeling of security and comfort. They do not resist like hard floors, chairs, and blocks. This responsiveness is what creates the internal calmness young children need to begin regulating strong emotions. Cover soft furnishings with pillowcases, sheets, duvet covers, or cinch sacks that can be removed easily for washing.

NOW TRY THIS! Making a Cozy Space

When creating a cozy space for your early learning setting, invite children to help design it.

1. Ask children to close their eyes to connect with the feeling of being in their cozy place at home.

2. Make comments and ask questions that help children connect to the feeling you're trying to achieve in this area of the early learning setting ("What part of your home is your favorite place to relax?," "Tell me about your bed at home").

3. Ask families to provide photos of children's bedrooms or quiet spaces at home (or objects from those spaces) to serve as a concrete materials to help inspire discussion.

4. During the conversation, introduce vocabulary like *fuzzy, fluffy, smooth*, and *squishy*.

5. Ask children to contribute ideas about how to make the space more comfortable and cozier, including materials that make them feel calm and balanced.

Preschoolers at Play

When children know that a space like this is available and are encouraged to use it, they will.

> As Ms. Huang moves from child to child in her preschool setting, asking children their plans for their center work, 4-year-old Joshua becomes upset. He takes deep breaths, a calming strategy he has been working on with Ms. Huang. When it is his turn to plan, Joshua says, "I'll be right back," and walks to the cozy area of the classroom. Instead of pressuring him to talk about why he is upset, Ms. Huang says, "Okay. Can you let me know when you feel ready to talk?" She then moves on to the next child. Periodically, Ms. Huang glances over at Joshua, who is now lying down on a blanket with his head propped up on a pillow. He has chosen his favorite stuffed dinosaur from the collection of stuffed animals, and she observes him whispering quietly to the dinosaur and practicing his deep breathing. After a few moments, Joshua comes back to Ms. Huang and says, "I'm ready now."

Cozy spaces, like the one used by Joshua, can be a safe haven for children who find the activity level of a typical learning setting overwhelming. Make sure the space is protected and away from more heavily trafficked or louder areas. Place the cozy space within view of where whole group activities occur. This lets a child observe what is happening from the comfort of the private area while also allowing the teacher to keep the child in sight.

While most early learning settings with a cozy space use it as a place where children can calm down when upset, encourage children to use it as a space to go to reflect on happiness as well. Promote it as a place for quiet reflection, no matter how the child is feeling.

Conclusion

Children enter preschool with a range of experiences in forming relationships, playing and interacting with others, and understanding their own emotions. Some children have only ever spent time with their parent or grandparent. Others have had many experiences being away from their primary caregiver and playing with many other children. All children's social and emotional learning and development can be supported no matter their prior experiences. Learning to manage emotions and self-regulate behaviors is no easy task for 3- to 5-year-olds, but teachers who carefully select play materials and offer consistent support can help children become more caring, compassionate, and cooperative.

TECH TIPS

- Take photos or videos of children working together and then review them with the children. Discuss with the children what they notice about their interactions and conversations.

- After reading a book on feelings, give children a digital camera and encourage them to take photos of how their faces look when they express different emotions.

- Create a chart with a variety of images on the smart board and encourage children to tap on the image that best represents their feelings.

- Download apps like Headspace that provide child-appropriate guided meditations. Place a tablet with this app in the cozy space of your early learning setting for children to use.

- Play audio recordings of people laughing, crying, squealing, and whining. Ask children what they think the person might be feeling.

Suggested Play Materials

Drawing and Painting

- Drawing materials of varying thicknesses (e.g., chalk, colored pencils, crayons, markers, nontoxic oil pastels)

- Paint of various types (e.g., finger paint, tempera, watercolor) and painting accessories (e.g., easels, paintbrushes in varying thicknesses, palettes, small sponges, unbreakable jars)

- Paper (e.g., construction paper in various colors, shapes, and sizes; textured paper; wallpaper samples, wrapping paper)

Sculpting and Crafting

- Adhesives (e.g., glue bottles and sticks, paste, tape)

- Craft materials for collaging (e.g., acrylic gemstones, chenille stems, craft sticks, crystals, fabric, paint chip samples, pom-poms, prisms)

- Light tables and overhead projectors

- Natural materials (e.g., acorns, bark, grass, leaves, pine cones, seashells, seedpods, small stones, twigs)

- Playdough and clay

- Recyclable materials for building and collaging (e.g., aluminum cans and foil, bottle caps, cardboard boxes and tubes, carpet and flooring samples, cotton balls, egg cartons, food containers, magazines, plastic bottles and jars, spools, straws, Styrofoam pieces)

- Tools (e.g., hole punchers, paper clips, scissors, staplers)

Art Appreciation and References

- Biographies of influential artists geared toward young children

- Children's books with interesting illustrations

- Fine art examples (e.g., mobiles, posters and prints of paintings, sculptures)

- Human and animal figures with poseable body parts that are realistically proportioned

CHAPTER 11

Play Materials That Invite My Creative Expression Through Visual Arts

The Reggio Emilia approach upholds that children have one hundred languages with which to communicate. These symbolic languages allow children to express themselves in many different ways, support children in wondering and creating, and promote the belief that there is no "right" or "wrong" way of expression (Edwards, Gandini, & Forman 1998). This chapter explores one of the languages that helps children express what they think and how they feel: the visual arts.

Art has long been considered a crucial form of expression in early childhood. Preschool standards recognize the importance of the creative arts (see Georgia Department of Early Care and Learning, n.d.; New Jersey Department of Education 2014). Visual art experiences support young children's learning and development in a wide range of areas, including cognitive development, social and emotional development, language development, fine motor skills, and creative problem solving. As preschoolers engage with play materials that stimulate their creative senses, they are given opportunities to demonstrate their understanding of the world. With thoughtful selections by and interactions with teachers, art play materials encourage children to explore, test boundaries, and use new approaches to learning.

Think about how play materials are arranged and displayed in your art learning center. Kneel or sit down in the center and experience how the area looks from the perspective of children as well as how it might *feel* for the children. A shelf that looks interesting and exciting to an adult might appear messy and inaccessible to a child. If you notice children are not visiting the art learning center much, evaluate how to change the presentation of play materials to spark their interest. Consider the descriptions in "Sending a Positive Message About Visual Arts" and think about how each would affect a child exploring art play materials.

Art play materials should give children opportunities to find their own creative voices. Open-ended materials invite children to explore the idea of change and how materials respond to input from their hands and the tools they use. As children explore and interact with play materials like playdough, paint, and colored pencils, pose challenges or ask questions. Try these questions, or come up with your own:

> "How do you think you could change the colors on this part of the painting without starting over?"

> "How could you make this part of your clay figure a little smoother in texture?"

> "You said you wanted your drawing of your mommy to have curly hair. What could you do to make her hair look curly?"

As children continue to develop verbal language and abstract thinking skills, asking them questions about their preferences and ideas helps make the knowledge they gain while engaging with play materials meaningful.

Sending a Positive Message About Visual Arts

Spaces That Welcome and Support Children's Artistic Expression	Spaces to Avoid
Paint cups are set up with clean brushes, palettes, and interesting paper nearby, ready for children to use independently.	Paint cups are tightly sealed and stored on a shelf away from paper and brushes. Brushes have dried paint on them.
Interesting collage materials are stored in small, labeled baskets that children can carry to the table. There are different kinds of paper and adhesives like tape and glue nearby.	Collage materials are kept in closed bags on a high shelf, at the back of a shelf behind other materials, or mixed together in a bin. The glue bottles are dried or empty and kept in a closed container next to the sink.
Soft, moldable playdough is accessible for children to use. Small baskets of tools like craft sticks, small figures, shells, and cookie cutters are on the shelf next to the playdough. Plastic placemats are available for each child to use, helping to define each child's space and to make clean up easier.	The playdough container is often left open, and the playdough is dried and crumbly. There are a few cookie cutters to use, and children tend to argue over the amount of playdough they have. The crumbled playdough usually ends up on the floor or all over the table.
There are a variety of items to choose from when painting at the easel including different-size paper, fabric, cardboard, or even old shoes and hats.	Teachers keep paper in a closed cabinet and children must ask for help before painting. There is plain white paper to use and only a few primary colors to choose from.

Visual art is mostly a process-based activity for preschoolers. The focus is on exploring materials and creating, not on the finished product. Encourage children to reflect on their process of creating by making comments and asking thoughtful questions. Be careful about using phrases like "That's so pretty!" or "I really like that" when commenting on children's artwork. Always remember that how *you* feel about a child's creative work is not important—it's how *the child* feels about it!

Paint and Painting Accessories

Painting in the early learning setting is like cooking in a kitchen: it's just meant to be! With the right space and materials, painting can be a relaxing, motivating, and educational experience. Incorporate different kinds of paint that children can use with different tools—including their fingers!—and on different mediums. In addition to more traditional painting tools like paintbrushes and small sponges, provide natural items like leaves and flowers. Children can dip these in paint and press them to paper or fabric to create print art. Encourage children to work on a painting in multiple stages. After they apply a base layer of paint, they might introduce details into the creation. This shows children that work can be started, reflected on, and changed.

Working with primary colors alone can be limiting to children. As children paint, have conversations about the colors of items they see outside or at home and encourage them to explore mixing paints to recreate shades of color found in the real world ("Look at the color of this hibiscus flower; I wonder if we can make a shade of pink that matches it," "Jasmin has such an interesting eye color. Do you think we could mix paints to make a shade of greenish-blue that matches them?"). Place palettes and unbreakable jars nearby and demonstrate how to mix and blend colors.

Paints that represent diverse skin tones give children the ability to explore visual similarities and differences among people. There are a number of brands that have paint sets (as well as other visual art play materials) developed especially for this purpose, including Colorations' Colors Like Me and Lakeshore's People Colors. By providing paints that reflect many skin tones, you send the message that everyone is accepted, recognized, and appreciated. It also gives children in early learning programs without much visible diversity in its community to see and develop an appreciation for people who look different than they do.

As you gather and offer painting materials, keep in mind the ages and abilities of the preschoolers you teach. For example, consider the size and shape of paper and brushes. Because young preschoolers tend to make large, irregular strokes while painting, the paper you provide should be big enough to accommodate their developing fine motor control. As fine motor skills improve, smaller pieces of paper or paper cut into different shapes can be offered. Invite

NOW TRY THIS! Exploring Color

- Scaffold children's vocabulary by using words like *tints, shades, lighter,* and *darker.*

- Introduce more sophisticated color names like *chartreuse, fuchsia,* and *turquoise.*

- When a child mixes several paints to make a new color, invite them to come up with their own special name for that color.

- Provide a variety of interesting natural objects children can look at as references or paint on while experimenting with color mixing.

children to cut out their own paper shape before they begin painting. Some children, including those with visual impairments or physical disabilities and delays, may also find it helpful for paper to be secured to an easel or placed inside a shirt box for extra stability (Brillante 2017).

Craft and Recyclable Materials for Collaging

Creating collages by selecting, arranging, and combining interesting materials engages children in creating art while learning more about properties like size, shape, and color. Collaging also invites children to explore spatial awareness, play with filling spaces, and figure out new relationships between objects.

As with other open-ended play materials, an exploration stage is necessary for young children to experiment with all of the potential uses for collage materials. When introducing consumable collage materials like pom-poms or acrylic gemstones, invite children to first explore them without adhesives like glue, paste, or tape. Without adhesives in the mix, children can focus on the properties and features of the collage materials themselves. Once adhesives are introduced, use them to scaffold learning and inspire problem-solving opportunities, such as deciding which adhesive is best for making each kind of material stick to a collage and determining how long each takes to apply or dry.

To extend young children's use of collage materials, provide a light table or overhead projector to arrange items on. Arranging items in creative ways on a light table offers a different and unique collage experience for children, opening up opportunities for plenty of high-level, creative thinking. Collaging on a light table or overhead projector also allows play materials to be used more than once, as each collage is created and then taken apart. Offer a variety of interesting materials—both familiar and new—to create these unfixed collages, including translucent items (e.g., acrylic gemstones, colored acrylic shapes, colored cellophane, unbreakable crystals and prisms) and opaque objects (e.g., chenille stems, fabrics, pom-poms). Encourage children to analyze and talk about how these play materials look different on the light table or overhead projector.

Fine Art Examples

Materials and displays that feature fine art from famous artists and illustrations from children's books expose children to different ways of making art and using art play materials. Introducing children to different art mediums and techniques broadens their perspectives on art, expands their ideas about how materials can be used, and encourages them to develop their own style of expression.

Hang posters or prints of paintings or create an inspiration book of works by artists like Ravi Mandlick, Torkwase Dyson, and Wassily Kandinsky near the easel. While discussing the artists' techniques, invite children to experiment with how they create art ("Did you notice how this artist used a lot of circles to create their painting? I wonder if you can try that too," "How do you think this artist created this painting? What tools do you think they used?"). When discussing fine art examples, introduce and use the proper terminology (e.g., *aesthetic, composition, multimedia*).

Children's books are another rich source of artwork that you and children can explore together. Faith Ringgold is a children's book author and illustrator who uses fabric, paint, and words to create her art. Eric Carle and Leo Lionni are known for their use of collage to illustrate their books. Mitsumasa Anno uses ink and watercolors to create his detailed illustrations. As you walk children through discussions about the art in their favorite books, consider asking these questions:

> "How do you think the illustrations were created?"

> "What materials do we have in the classroom that look like the ones the illustrator used?"

> "What do you like best about these illustrations?"

To scaffold children's explorations of different styles and use of materials, engage a small group of children in a study of a children's book author/illustrator (like Faith Ringgold or Simms Taback) or a painter or sculptor (like Mary Lovelace O'Neal or Alexander Calder). Offer several examples of their art and lead children through a long-term study.

Multimedia artworks, in particular, encourage children to be flexible in their thinking about art materials and ways of using them. They provide the opportunity to introduce multistep projects to children, sending the message that it is okay to work on something and go back to it several times, adding details and changing it as they go along. Older preschoolers will be especially curious about these multistep projects and challenged by creating something over multiple days.

Conclusion

Visual art is a form of expression—a language. Aside from supporting children in discovering the importance of aesthetics (or the principles of artistic beauty), art play materials encourage expression and communication of thoughts, feelings, and understandings of the world. As children progress through stages of artistic representation, they begin by exploring the very concrete properties of color, line, and shape. Artwork becomes more representational as children find meaning in what they are creating. At higher levels of mastery, children can connect their artwork to abstract concepts like emotion and thought. Often, young children do not have the verbal language to communicate what is in their minds and hearts, yet it comes through in their artwork. Consistent exposure to a variety of interesting play materials allows this skill to improve and children's artistic language to develop.

TECH TIPS

- Photograph colors children create with a tablet or smartphone and do a reverse Google search to discover what the name of the shade is.

- Take photos of children as they create art and display them beside the completed works.

- Introduce programs like Microsoft Paint, apps like Draw it, or websites like Tate Paint for children to explore artmaking through a digital medium.

- Use a Sphero robot synced with the Sphero Draw app to bring drawings to life. Children can draw a design on the tablet and the Sphero robot will follow their virtual design.

- Connect a smart board to a document camera so that children can view their collages on a large screen and examine the materials they are using in detail. Several children might work on one collage together, fostering cooperation and collaboration.

- Explore the work of famous artists and children's book illustrators online. Many museum websites include virtual galleries where art can be viewed (e.g., Children's Museum of the Arts, The Eric Carle Museum of Picture Book Art).

Suggested Play Materials

Creative Movement and Dance

- Beanbags
- Dance costumes and accessories (e.g., feather boas, leotards, tap shoes, tutus)
- Handheld dance props (e.g., glow sticks, long streamers, pom-poms, ribbons, scarves)
- Hula-Hoops

Sound, Voice, and Vibration

- CD/MP3 players and devices that can access online music libraries
- Electronic instruments (e.g., drum pad with sticks, keyboard with synthetic sounds)
- Microphones and wireless speakers
- Percussion instruments (e.g., castanets, güiros, maracas, mbiras, rainsticks, rhythm sticks, sand blocks, talking drums, tambourines, triangles, xylophones)
- Recorded music of various cultures, genres, and languages (e.g., bachata, blue grass, bossa nova, classical, electronic, hip-hop, jazz, nature sounds, nursery rhymes, reggae, salsa, Tejano)
- Recycled, natural, or nontraditional materials that produce sound when combined and manipulated (e.g., C-shaped PVC pieces for blowing or singing into, rubber bands stretched over tissue boxes for strumming, seedpods in sealed plastic containers for shaking, smooth stones to hit together like cymbals, sticks for tapping together)
- Stringed instruments (e.g., banjos, harps, mini guitars, ukuleles)

Creating Visual Representations of Music

- Color-coded songbooks
- Materials for drawing or writing music (e.g., colored pencils, dot markers, lined and unlined paper, rulers, stickers)
- Sheet music

CHAPTER 12

Play Materials That Encourage Me to Explore and Make Music

Music is a language, even without words. Rhythms ebb and flow, tones go up and down, and patterns emerge. Similar to the way you speak to children, the musical play materials and experiences you introduce convey messages, moods, and emotions. Whether you are introducing the soothing sound of a rainstick or discussing the different layers of classical and electronica music, each song and sound says something. It is up to you and the children to explore what exactly that message is.

When thinking about which music play materials to incorporate in your early learning setting, consider the variety of experiences each material can provide, both in self-directed and teacher-guided play; for example

> Engaging in creative expression

> Community building

> Performing for and being part of an audience

> Exploring cause-and-effect relationships

> Identifying patterns in rhythms

> Comparing and contrasting

Early childhood teachers sometimes have varying opinions about their own musical skills. Regardless of how you feel about your own abilities, music can and should be part of every preschool environment. Encourage children to share musical memories by asking questions ("What do you think about when you hear this sound? Does it remind you of anything?," "Where do you hear music when you're with your family? In the house? In the car? At the store?"). Invite families to share information about family songs or common experiences with music. Find a recording of a lullaby a family has shared with you and play it for the class.

Younger preschoolers may focus more on music's sensations, vibrations, and tones and pay less attention to the details of music and the emotions that music inspires. As children get older, they become more aware of the feelings that music evokes and can explore ways to represent their emotions through music (Eerola, Friberg, & Bresin 2013). A sense of community develops as children engage in musical experiences, dance, and laugh next to one another. They share in the excitement of singing, moving to, and making music.

Recorded Music of Various Cultures, Genres, and Languages

Music from different genres and cultures exposes children to a variety of tempos, rhythms, instruments, vocabulary, and dance moves. Some musical selections will be new to children, while others may be similar to what they have heard outside of the early learning setting. This balance introduces children to sounds and songs they are unfamiliar with while also helping children to connect their classroom community to experiences at home. For example, a child who listens to reggae music with their older cousins may be able to share a few accompanying dance moves with their peers, and a Tejano song may inspire another child to tell a story about the family parties where they usually hear this kind of music.

In a quiet corner of the early learning setting, set up a listening center with music players and sets of headphones. This encourages children to listen to music independently during self-directed play without adding to the volume of the overall space or distracting other children from their

NOW TRY THIS! Shared Musical Experiences

Invite children to play one musical instrument with a partner (e.g., one child holds a tambourine while another child taps it with a finger) or to play an instrument while their peers move and dance to the music they create.

You can celebrate the collaboration or prompt discussion by making comments like

■ "Tony and Kamil, you both worked together really well to make a drumbeat. You make a great band!"

■ "Thank you for playing music so Cierra could dance to it. Your performance together was beautiful."

■ "I noticed the way Johan moves the pom-poms matches the way you shake the tambourine. When you go slow, he goes slow; when you go fast, so does he. I wonder why that is."

play. While online music streaming services are used by more tech-forward early learning programs, MP3 players, CDs, and even audio cassettes remain in frequent use by many teachers. When organizing physical music formats like CDs and audio cassettes in the listening center, label each with a one- or two-word title and a symbol that represents the song or kind of music it is. If you're not sure what symbol to use, play a piece of music during a whole group time and invite the children to choose one. As an alternative, download favorite songs onto a tablet and create shortcuts using a familiar symbol and the name of the song. For example, you might find a picture of a small spider and include the name "Itsy Bitsy Spider" under it so children can identify the song more easily.

Set up specific guidelines and rules for children to keep in mind as they handle recorded music materials. You might show children how to hold a CD by putting a finger into the small hole in the center or explain how they should avoid touching the tape in an audio cassette so as not to damage it. Describe what the symbols on the buttons of MP3, CD, and audio cassette players mean so that children understand how to operate them ("One arrow pointing to the right means play. Two arrows pointing to the right means fast-forward"). You can also place colored stickers on the buttons ("There is a green sticker on the play button; green means go"). Repeat the guidelines for properly handling these materials throughout the year as preschoolers develop their independence and self-regulation skills.

Tips for Literacy Connections

■ When introducing a new song to children, write the lyrics on a poster board to put on display. You might write the lyrics in rebus form, replacing some of the words with simple drawings or pictures. Children can read along as you point out rhyming words, familiar sight words, and repeating phrases.

■ Read a poem to music or find a prerecorded version. Adding music to poetry reading heightens the rhythmic nature and gives children a unique experience with poetry.

While it's not recommended to have loud music playing in the background throughout the day (Harms, Clifford, & Cryer, 2014), engaging children in activities with music and other play materials can prompt some serious thinking. Play instrumental music near easels or at a table where a small group of children paint. Encourage children to "paint the music"—that is, to visually show how the music makes them feel or what it makes them think of—and discuss their work afterward. Observe what is happening: Do children's strokes intensify with faster-paced music? Do they slow down with the rhythm? These observations can be helpful in learning how children interpret information and how they are responding to music as a modality for learning. For older children with more developed fine motor skills, play a song with lyrics and invite them to choose their favorite drawing material to "draw the music." While painting may lead to broad strokes, you may be surprised to find the detail children include in their work with a simple switch of materials. For more information on this play experience, see "Materials for Drawing or Writing Music" later in this chapter.

Percussion Instruments

Percussion instruments give young children the chance to explore sound in unique and interesting ways. Depending on the instrument, sounds are produced differently. Some instruments are played by being shaken or pressed with your hands while others are struck, rubbed, or scraped with a stick or mallet. Include a variety of percussion instruments to suit the developmental abilities and needs of the children you teach. Younger preschoolers will most likely be more comfortable with instruments they can grasp, shake, and hit, such as maracas, bells, and hand drums. Older preschoolers generally have greater dexterity, and to meet the needs of their more advanced fine motor skills, you can provide instruments like castanets (finger cymbals) and xylophones. Adapt and modify instruments to support children with delays or disabilities in engaging with them; for example, if a child can shake their arms but not grasp an object, add wrist or arm straps. As children become more familiar with percussion instruments, expand the selection available to include electronic and stringed instruments.

Use the correct names for instruments, but encourage children to make up their own! Engage in a discussion with children comparing the different ways instruments can be played. The emphasis here is on not figuring out what is "right" or "wrong," just what is different. Try these questions:

> "How does this drum sound when you shake it around? How about this rainstick?"

> "How do the rhythm sticks sound different when you hit them together compared to when you rub them together?"

> "When you put that bell on your ankle instead of your wrist, do you think it sounds different? How? What other body parts could you play the bell with?"

> "What kind of instrument can you make using materials in our classroom?"

Just like other play materials, there should be ample time for children to explore and play with musical instruments. Depending on children's past experiences with instruments at home or in the early learning setting, they will either be very focused and intentional while using them or simply experiment with the sounds they make. Support children to use instruments individually, in small groups, and in large groups. In addition to developing a musical awareness when using instruments, children can also work on their interpersonal skills, such as turn-taking, communicating, negotiating, and problem solving (Fox & Liu 2012).

Place a small- to medium-size rug next to a shelf big enough to display instruments in an inviting way. When space or furniture is limited, hang a plastic or fabric shoe rack on the wall and store one instrument in each pocket or on each hook. You might also include a label with the picture and name of the instrument so children can put them away independently. Encourage children to use the music center independently as well as engage in teacher-initiated music experiences.

Some children can become overstimulated during loud activities, so observe how children react while there is music happening in the room. Introducing percussion instruments during a small or whole group time gives you the opportunity to observe these reactions. If you see a child covering their ears or becoming agitated, offer them a set of headphones to muffle the sound. This is especially important when engaging in whole group music experiences, during which the sound can be louder. Place instruments in the louder part of the learning setting, such as near the dramatic play and block centers, keeping them separated from the quieter centers for book reading and visual artmaking (Harms, Clifford, & Cryer 2014). Inspire critical thinking by shaking things up! Bring instruments from the learning setting into the bathroom, gym, auditorium, or even outdoors. Introduce the word *acoustics* as you and the children play each instrument and discuss how the sound changes from area to area.

Children can also use music as a vehicle for communication. Most basic percussion instruments require very little fine motor coordination, but much like words, they offer a wide variety of sounds with which to communicate. For example, you might ask a child a question and demonstrate how to respond *yes* or *no* using two different instruments, one to represent each answer. In using instruments this way, connections to music develop and children may be able to express a broader range of emotions, thoughts, and opinions. Scaffold the idea of communicating with instruments by leading children through a storytelling activity where different percussion instruments represent different characters, as in Sergei Prokofiev's *Peter and the Wolf*. Children can become active participants in a story you are telling or be guided through inventing their own story.

Nature Sounds and Making Instruments with Natural Materials

> While Mr. Parnassus's preschoolers are out on the playground, he notices 3-year-old Sarai standing alone under a tree, looking up at the leaves. Mr. Parnassus approaches Sarai, kneels down next to her, and follows her gaze into the tree. Sarai looks at her teacher, wide-eyed with excitement. "The bird is talking!"
>
> Mr. Parnassus smiles. "Yes, he's singing, just like you do in class. What other sounds do you hear?"
>
> Sarai looks back up at the tree. "I hear the tree," she replies. Mr. Parnassus recognizes the teachable moment to extend her vocabulary. "You hear the leaves rustling in the wind. I can also hear the water in that little stream behind the fence. It's like the birds and the trees and the water are making music together!" says Mr. Parnassus.
>
> He takes out the classroom tablet from his bag and records the sounds they are hearing to play them back later in the classroom. Mr. Parnassus plans to introduce Sarai to the instrument-making area in their music center, where she can choose some natural items to play along with the sounds of nature.

Thinking and talking about the nature sounds that children observe outside as music can go hand-in-hand with making instruments from natural materials. Fill a box with natural items like seashells, leaves, twigs, stones, sand, and seedpods. Add cardboard boxes and tubes, plastic jars, and envelopes nearby so children can fill them with natural items and explore combinations of sounds. Point out how different materials make different sounds, and encourage children to compare which have sharper or flatter sounds. Note the combinations children create and give them opportunities to explain why they think certain materials make certain sounds.

You can extend children's thinking about nature sounds as music with questions like

- "How many stones did you put inside of this jar? How does it sound? I wonder what would happen if you added more (put in fewer) stones."

- "Which of the instruments you made sounds like the maraca in the music center?"

- "How does the sound change when you put twigs inside the jar instead of sand? Describe it."

- "What other container could you use to hold the leaves to change the sound? Let's experiment!"

- "Which sound do you think might be nice for when you're relaxing?"

- "What kind of song could we make while you shake that box full of seedpods and I slide around this envelope of sand?"

Materials for Drawing or Writing Music

Have you ever wondered how children might "see" or visualize music? Creating a visual representation of what they are hearing is a high-level way of exploring the language of music. You can incorporate materials to explore drawing or writing music into the music center; however, an intentional introduction to using the materials in this specific way is needed. Start by gathering a small group of children at the table or on the rug. Have available basic percussion instruments (e.g., hand drums, triangles, rhythm sticks, tambourines) and writing materials (e.g., paper, markers, colored pencils, dot painters). Play a simple beat with one instrument, keeping a slow, steady rhythm. Invite the children to choose a color from the available materials to represent the sound on paper.

Start with a slow beat as children begin to recognize the connection between the sound and drawing. Play the beat for 20 to 30 seconds, and encourage each child to make a mark on their paper every time the instrument makes a sound or your hand moves. Acknowledge and celebrate any attempt at creating marks on their paper ("I see you making a blue mark on your paper every time my hand comes down"). After you've played the beat for a few minutes and observed children following along, pause and ask them what they see on their paper ("How many marks did you make on your paper?," "Tell me about what you're doing").

Extend the activity by asking the group which instrument you should choose next, and let them know they can pick a different color for this next sound. You might vary the speed this time, playing it a little faster. Observe each child's body language as they progress through this activity to determine whether you can add another instrument. If they are engaged and enjoying the experiment, you might add a third instrument, playing an even faster rhythm on this one.

After you've repeated this process with two or three instruments, discuss what the children have put down on paper. Encourage them to look at one another's papers to see what others have done. Ask questions such as

❭ "What do you notice about the blue dots and the yellow dots on Angie's paper?"

❭ "Why do you think there are so many more red strokes than green ones?"

❭ "Why did you choose the color blue to show the drumbeat?"

This activity is a unique way to explore instruments, rhythm and tempo, and patterns with young children. Try it more than once, either individually or in small groups as children get the hang of it. Always ask the children how they are feeling about the activity and if they want to continue. As children become more experienced with this process, they might try using a piece of recorded music to further their explorations of writing or drawing music.

Conclusion

Music is a powerful tool for helping young children learn new concepts and extending their understanding of concepts they are already familiar with. Used with intention, purpose, and joy, music adds richness to the experiences you provide for children and the learning environment you create together. Music can enhance children's engagement with play materials and inspire new ways of thinking about them. This chapter offered many suggestions for comments and questions. However, if you observe a child deep in enjoyment while making, dancing to, or listening to music, avoid interrupting their explorations and let them be fully immersed in the experience. That's the beauty of the language of music: sometimes, you don't need words.

TECH TIPS

- Using YouTube and other online resources, find and watch videos of people from around the world singing songs, playing instruments, and dancing to music that are part of their cultural heritage. After watching them with children, discuss the similarities and differences they noticed.

- Use a smartphone, tablet, or other device capable of recording video to capture children singing, playing instruments, or dancing. Watch the video with children and discuss what they observe.

- Offer an electronic keyboard with synthetic sounds, and ask children to compare the sound the keyboard makes with the real instrument (e.g., the synthetic drumbeat the keyboard produces with the drumbeat from an actual drum). Discuss why they might sound different from each other.

- Use music notation software, such as ScoreCloud, so children can see what a favorite song looks like on paper.

Suggested Play Materials

Role-Playing

- Bags (e.g., backpacks, briefcases, gourds, purses, reusable grocery bags, waist packs, woven baskets)

- Dolls and doll accessories and furniture (e.g., blankets, car seats, clothing, cribs, diapers, high chairs, wheelchairs)

- Dress-up clothing and accessories (e.g., collared shirts, dresses, hats, jewelry, skirts, sunglasses, ties), including some that represent diversity in age and ability (e.g., ankle and wrist braces, arm slings, eyeglasses with lenses removed, hearing aids); traditional clothing from various cultures (e.g., dashikis, embroidered items, hanboks, kilts, kimonos, moccasins, saris, sombreros); and uniforms for work roles (e.g., aprons, blazers, hard hats, jerseys, scrubs, spacesuit helmets)

- Equipment and items for specific dramatic play scenarios (e.g., cash registers and baskets for grocery shopping, tents and flashlights for camping)

- Household accessories, appliances (nonfunctioning and with cords removed), and furniture, both real and pretend (e.g., baking sheets, bamboo steamer baskets, dishes and utensils for eating and serving, oven mitts, pots and pans, rolling pins, small table and chairs, tortilla press, washing machine and dryer)

Imaginative and Symbolic Thinking

- Fabrics and textiles of varying sizes (e.g., cotton quilting fabrics, lace curtain panels, sheer scarves, tablecloths, traditional prints from various cultures)

- Literacy materials (e.g., computer keyboard with the cord cut, grocery store circulars, laminated newspapers, menus from a variety of restaurants, paper and blank booklets, pencils and crayons, recipe books)

- Play food made of wood or molded plastic and craft materials or natural items to represent food (e.g., acorns, playdough, pom-poms, river stones)

- Recyclables (e.g., cardboard boxes and tubes, empty food boxes and cartons, seasoning shakers)

CHAPTER 13

Play Materials That Inspire Pretend Play and Dramatic Play

Dramatic play is a powerful vehicle for preschoolers to learn lessons about social roles: how people care for one another, the jobs they do, and how they respect and support their community and environment. Three- to 5-year-olds are constantly learning how to negotiate roles, navigate peer relationships, and develop ways to express what they understand—or are trying to understand—about the world. Around 5-years-old, children are developing the ability to see different perspectives and realizing that others might have a different opinion of the same experience (NAEYC 2022). Through dramatic play, children can develop their identity and understand how they fit into the world around them.

Children's pretend play and choice of play materials reveal their understanding of relationships. When children gravitate toward certain dramatic play roles, it can be a peek into how they understand what that role means to them. For example, teachers might hear two children shout, "No, I want to be the mommy!" Consider how to navigate this by thinking about the play materials the children are using. If it is a special sequined dress or flowered skirt that children argue only "the mommy" wears, add a few other similar clothing options the children can use to potentially explore other roles. If it is a doll that several children want to take care of, make sure there are multiple dolls or stuffed animals available for children to care for. Alternately, invite children to consider the possibility of a baby having two mommies and invite them to think about what it means to be a caregiver. By engaging in cooperative play and with guidance from teachers, children learn how to identify real problems and create solutions that work for everyone.

Intentional conversations about children's use of play materials also helps children develop awareness of the similarities and differences in their personal characteristics, experiences, customs, family roles, and more (Kamdar 2020).

Preschool teacher Ms. Arguelles observes Zoë and Xavier, both age 4, playing together in the dramatic play center. She watches Xavier carry a baby doll to the table and wrap a small cloth around the baby's bottom. He sings softly to the doll while he arranges the cloth.

Zoë watches him carefully, puts her hand on her hip, and states matter-of-factly, "What you doing? Daddies don't do the diapers!"

Ms. Arguelles remembers right away that Xavier's mother is a nurse and works nights. His father gets him and his baby brother ready for bed each night. Instead of getting angry at Zoë for chastising her friend, Ms. Arguelles starts a discussion about how different families work to take care of one another. She helps them understand the concept of family diversity in the context of relationships and what each person brings to the family. She also invites them to explore the characteristics of their own families and how each individual relates to one another, no matter what gender each person is.

Family roles, such as a consistent babysitter or grandparent, might also find their way into children's dramatic play. Any person a child identifies as part of their family unit should be honored, respected, and celebrated as an important relationship in that child's life.

Pay close attention to how the dramatic play center works for children. It should be the hub for all role-playing. If children are moving materials into the block center to create a picnic, consider how you can change the dramatic play center to accommodate the needs of the play. Notice when children do move materials around the room and make sure it is not disrupting the play specific to the other learning centers.

If children seem to be arguing over or mishandling play materials or engaging in unfocused play, take a look at what materials are available; for example

> If children argue over the same brightly colored shirt, consider whether there are enough appealing items of clothing to interest the children.

NOW TRY THIS! Shake Things Up

The dramatic play center is an evolving and fluid space. Children can become bored using the same play materials that have been available for long periods of time, and you may notice that the once-busy center is now rarely visited. While some staple play materials should always be available (e.g., household accessories and appliances, dolls), regularly refresh the space to suit the children's current interests and investigations. For example, after a visit to a nearby flower shop, you might modify the dramatic play center by

- Including fake flowers, vases, foam cubes, a cash register, and some books about flowers

- Asking the florist for some of their outdated catalogs and order forms

- Encouraging children to go to the art center and make their own props to support their dramatic play

> If there is an abundance of play food, are there pots, pans, and utensils to use with the food? Children may be having a difficult time incorporating the food into their play without the accessories.

> If there are four tubs filled with various bags, consider putting out only two tubs. This may be less overwhelming for children and help to focus their play.

Dolls and Doll Accessories and Furniture

Provide dolls that represent a range of skin tones as well as different facial features and hair textures. Children need opportunities to play with dolls that look like themselves and also ones that don't.

Doll play supports cognitive, physical, and social and emotional learning and development (Hashmi et al. 2021):

> Dolls encourage children to experiment and take on family and community roles. Children can pretend to be a primary caregiver feeding their baby or a doctor caring for a sick infant. (Social and emotional)

> Children practice their interpersonal skills by communicating their ideas to others and collaborating on how the dolls fit into their pretend play scenarios. (Social and emotional)

> Buttoning pants, zipping up a dress, and pulling a shirt over a doll's head gives children opportunities to practice their fine motor and spatial awareness skills. (Physical and cognitive)

> Doll play inspires children to use familiar and new vocabulary associated with caretaking and family life. (Cognitive)

> Pretending to change a doll's diaper, putting the baby to sleep, or feeding them healthy foods helps children become aware of their own bodily needs and functions. (Physical)

> Children can express and model emotions through dolls in a way that feels safe. (Social and emotional)

Taking care of babies is one of the things that makes us all similar as humans, regardless of race, ethnicity, or socioeconomic status. Younger preschoolers might begin to interact with dolls by linking a series of actions ("First you put the baby in the high chair, then you take the food out, then finally you feed the baby"). This kind of play supports high-level perspective

taking, a key developmental shift during the preschool years (Hashmi et al. 2021). During doll play, the *child* is the responsible caregiver, quite a different experience than most 3- to 5-year-olds are used to. They have the opportunity to take on the adult role and have control over the dolls' lives the same way families have control over their lives. Draw attention to this important shift in perspective ("You're making the baby food. Who makes you food at home?," "You're taking care of the baby just like your grandma takes care of you after school"). Caring for a doll also gives teachers the opportunity to provide and connect vocabulary to the sensations associated with physical needs ("The baby is hungry; that means she needs food. How do you know when *you* are hungry?"). Through these play scenarios, you can also introduce American Sign Language signs for applicable words, such as *hungry* and *more*.

If you observe children putting dolls in "dangerous" situations, this type of play should be considered carefully. While teachers might instinctively want to stop controversial play, dramatic play with dolls is an outlet for children. It is important to allow certain play scenarios to unfold in order for children to explore real emotions, roles, and situations. "Too often, dramatic play themes are chosen by adults to allow children to practice safe, familiar roles (e.g., community helpers, housekeeping), while the emotionally engaging themes involving the struggle between good and evil, and courage in the face of danger, are actively discouraged, especially when the play script involves bad guys" (Logue & Detour 2011). Consider not stopping the play and instead using it as an opportunity to open conversations with the children about real and pretend. If this type of play happens repeatedly, it might be a clue that some deeper discussion is needed with families and other support members at your early learning program.

Fabrics and Textiles

Across the world and in every type of community, fabrics and textiles are used for different purposes. In their homes, children may see tablecloths, curtains, and towels. Blankets can be used on beds, for picnics, and sometimes even to divide up living spaces in a house. Children might notice fabric being used to carry babies or as a bag for groceries. Including fabrics in the dramatic play center opens the door for infinite possibilities.

Depending on the thickness and weave of a fabric, children might place it over their heads or cover a table with it. Start a conversation by saying, "Tell me about how this piece feels (looks). What do you feel (see)?" This helps children focus on the features and qualities of the fabric and encourages them to engage in higher-level thinking about the material.

As children experiment with wrapping pieces of fabric, strategically provide other items they might use to hold the fabric in place. Binder clips or bobby pins can be used to secure a dress or headwrap. For children with less refined fine motor skills, include large plastic clothespins that are easier to squeeze. Demonstrate how to tuck in fabric edges to make it stay in place or tie the ends together, relating it to tying shoelaces. To promote problem solving, you might ask, "How do you think these clips could be important while you're making your dress?" or comment, "I wonder what we could use to get the fabric to stay on your head." Other questions you could ask to extend children's thinking include

> "What did you do first (next, last) to put this on your body (your head, the doll)?"

> "What are some other places you've seen this kind of fabric? How do we use fabric in our houses (in class)?"

> "How is this fabric different from (the same as) the clothes you wore to school?"

> "How could we use this fabric in the art center (block center, outside)? Let's experiment!"

> "What's your favorite piece of fabric we have here? Why?"

> "Can you come up with a brand new way to use this fabric for carrying blocks (books, dolls)?"

Displaying photos that feature people from various cultures using fabric in different ways can inspire children to try new ideas. More important, it teaches them that there is no right or wrong way to use this play material. Get to know the children's families and their cultures, and provide fabrics that are familiar to the children. You might add silky saris, lace curtains, and Kente cloths.

The patterns and textures of fabrics can also inspire rich conversations about printing techniques, sewing, and how clothing is made. Ask questions like the following:

> "How do you think this pattern was made?"

> "What materials do you think were used to create it?"

> "What could you use to design your own pattern on this plain piece of fabric?"

Children might want to recreate a bògòlanfini (also known as a mud cloth) in the art center or try their hand at embroidering a piece of burlap with a large plastic needle. (For a more detailed discussion on sewing materials, see Chapter 15.) Cut plain white fabric (e.g., sheets from a secondhand store) into several pieces and place them near easels or on tables while children are painting or stamping. This piece of fabric art can later be used in the dramatic play center.

When children are done using the fabrics, introduce the concept of folding, using vocabulary like *corner, edge, triangle*, and *rectangle*. As they begin to understand the sequence of folding, you might ask, "Can you show me what you did to put the fabric away?" to see if children can recall and articulate the steps they took.

Recyclable Materials

Young children's thinking is often very concrete when they are first introduced to recyclable materials in the dramatic play center. They might engage with the materials only in contexts where they have seen them used before and already understand; cardboard boxes, for example, will make an appearance in play scenarios at the post office, while moving to a new home, or at a grocery store. Acknowledge when children recognize a recyclable material from their everyday lives (e.g., a cardboard tube from a paper towel roll as something they have seen in their kitchen at home) and ask questions that will inspire more flexible and symbolic thinking about the material ("What else does it remind you of?," "What happens when you look through one end?").

As children are ready, encourage more imaginary play using recyclables, such as attaching a cardboard box to a chair to create a shopping cart. (Put tennis balls on the feet of the chair or otherwise wrap them to protect the floor as children push them around.) If recyclable materials are available in another learning center, make sure the children understand that they may use them in the dramatic play center to support their play. Gradually, preschoolers will engage in more representational play independently, such as using aluminum can as a cup or an empty pasta box as a booster seat for a stuffed animal. To encourage this kind of creative thinking and problem solving, remove a favorite prop from the dramatic play center and see what happens!

> During center time in Ms. Repton's older preschool classroom, she notices four children in the dramatic play center chattering excitedly and looking puzzled. She walks to the center and sits down. "You look a little confused," she comments. "What's going on?"
>
> "The baby bed!" exclaims 5-year-old Jorge, motioning with his hands to the empty space where the crib is usually kept.
>
> "It looks like there's something missing from here," Ms. Repton says. "What do you notice?"
>
> "The baby's bed isn't here," 4-year-old Gretchen interjects.
>
> Knowing the crib was one of the children's favorite dramatic play props, Ms. Repton had taken it out of the center the day before to see what they might do. "You're right, the crib is missing. I wonder what you can do about that."
>
> Gretchen shrugs her shoulders, "Maybe we can make it."
>
> "Good thinking!" her teacher encourages. "Try looking around for some things you can use to make one."
>
> When Ms. Repton checks in with this group a little while later, she is pleased to find that they are laying the dolls down for a nap in cozy beds made from egg cartons.

With time, exposure, and intentional interactions with teachers and their peers, children will move into more advanced phases of symbolic play and begin to imagine and use recyclable materials more abstractly and with greater frequency. Suddenly, a cardboard box might go from being a washing machine to a rocket ship to a doghouse in the space of a single afternoon.

Conclusion

Observing children engaged in dramatic play allows early childhood educators to understand who children are and how children see themselves within family roles and friendships. Through this kind of play, children process emotions like empathy, compassion, and even anger and frustration. The dramatic play center should provide a mix of familiar and unfamiliar materials. Choosing play materials that represent the diversity of the children in your early learning setting as well as diversity beyond the classroom community is important for meeting the individual needs of children and encouraging their role-playing and symbolic thinking. Children gain insight into home routines and customs that differ from their own. When children work together in the dramatic play center, they are learning skills far beyond what the adults in the classroom can teach them.

TECH TIPS

- Using YouTube and other online resources, find and watch videos of families from different cultures doing daily household routines (e.g., preparing and eating a meal, taking care of a baby).

- Place a computer or other device loaded with a word-processing program in the dramatic play center for play scenarios that take place at work or in school.

- Provide a working calculator and cash register for play scenarios at the grocery store.

- Record children acting out a story, including all phases of the activity (e.g., reading the story, negotiating roles, creating props, rehearsing, performing). Watch the video with children and foster a reflective discussion about their process.

- Watch a cooking video with children and invite the children to follow along with the recipe by adding the ingredients (pretend food or recyclable materials representing the ingredients) to their dish.

Summary and Reflection

Providing play materials that support social and emotional learning and development is a foundational component of early childhood programs. Play experiences with carefully selected play materials help children build the language they need for understanding and regulating their emotions and interactions with others. Art, music, and dramatic play materials give children various avenues to express and communicate their ideas and feelings about the world. Encourage children to represent their emotions through art and color. Help them see music as a language to interact and celebrate with peers. Support them through dramatic play scenarios that mirror real-life relationships and conflicts.

. . . .

Now Ask Yourself This

- What are some things you do for self-care?

- How do the play materials in your early learning setting support the children to care for themselves?

- How do you celebrate when things go well?

- What rituals and traditions do you have in place for celebrating with the children you teach when things go well for them or others?

- What makes you feel good about who you are?

- How are diversity, creativity, and uniqueness acknowledged in your early learning program?

PART FOUR

Physical Learning and Development

Watching a child makes it obvious
that the development of his mind
comes through his movements.

—Maria Montessori, *The Absorbent Mind*

Suggested Play Materials

Endurance

- Hula-Hoops
- Jump ropes
- Swings
- Trampolines
- Tricycles and standing and seated scooters

Strength

- Elevated bars for hanging or pulling up on
- Materials for pushing, pulling, or transporting objects (e.g., laundry baskets, lawn mowers, wagons)
- Objects weighing 2 to 6 pounds for heavy lifting (e.g., containers filled with sand, pebbles, and water; dumbbells; kettlebells; medicine balls)
- Parachutes
- Ramps for walking, running, or peddling up

Balance

- Balance beams (e.g., curved, floor, textured) and stepping stones
- Collections of flat smooth items to walk on (e.g., foam circles, tree cookies, wooden blocks)
- Stilts
- Unstable yet safe walking surfaces (e.g., hinged bridges or slacklines installed 1 to 2 feet from the ground, large rocks, rounded logs)

Coordination and Cross-Lateral Movement

- Balls of various sizes and weights
- Ladders and stairs
- Obstacle courses (e.g., low hurdles, monkey bars, tires)
- Rackets, sticks, and pool noodles for striking balls or balloons
- Rock climbing walls
- Scoops (with and without balls attached)
- Steering wheels
- Tunnels

CHAPTER 14

Play Materials That Build My Gross Motor Skills

Vigorous physical activity has many benefits for young children. It increases balance, muscle coordination, endurance, and cardiovascular health (CDC, n.d. a). Gross motor activity—in other words, whole body movement that involves the large muscles of the arms, legs, or torso—also introduces children to a lifestyle that encourages exercise and promotes healthy choices. During vigorous physical activity, children will breathe heavier than normal, bringing more oxygen into their bodies to allow for increased focus and clearer thinking (Bidzan-Bluma & Lipowska 2018).

Children need plenty of opportunities to develop their large muscles and coordination skills, both indoors and out. Whether you have a large outdoor play space, an indoor gym, or some floor space in your early learning setting available, play materials that engage gross motor functions should be a part of children's daily experiences. Some of the skills and movements to consider when choosing play materials include balancing, jumping, rolling, tossing, catching, striking, crawling, kicking, and leaping.

Overall, young children show different levels of competency in gross motor skills mostly because of differences in experience. Consider how often they get to exercise while at home. Some research shows that there is an important relationship between how well a young child can perform a task and how they well they *think* they are performing it. Feelings of success can drive a child's motivation to continue working on the skill. Providing children with early wins (or small objectives that can be accomplished quickly and with relative ease) goes a long way in motivating them to continue trying (Stodden et al. 2012).

Children with physical delays and disabilities can be supported by their peers who have a more developed skill set. They might help a peer to lift, pull, or push a heavy object;

hold a ball still while their peer is attempting to kick it; or reach out a hand to support a child who is learning to balance. Just like any other skill, teachers must scaffold children's learning in gross motor development.

Objects for Heavy Lifting

Play materials that encourage children to engage in heavy lifting can be incorporated into your early learning setting's collection of portable gross motor resources. There is, of course, equipment that is specifically made for heavy lifting and available to purchase (e.g., dumbbells, kettlebells, medicine balls); however, making "heavy lifters" out of recyclable and found materials is a creative, no-cost way of bringing this strength-building activity to the children you teach (Craft & Smith 2010). Save gallon-size milk and water jugs and fill them with various materials (e.g., cotton balls, gravel, pebbles, sand, water), depending on how heavy you wish to make them. The large handle on the plastic jugs is ideal for small hands. Set aside a special area for using these play materials, separate from areas used for climbing, running, and wheeled toys.

When you observe children attempting to push, pull, or lift heavy objects, teach them proper technique to minimize the chance of accidents or injuries. Start with empty boxes or jugs and demonstrate how to first stand close to an object, get a firm grip on it, and then bend at the knees to lift. Continue helping them remember these steps ("When you picked up that box from the ground, what was the first thing you did with your legs and arms? Second? Last?"). A preschooler's ability to hold onto an object will also depend on small muscle development in their hands, so incorporating these objects can have benefits for both the large and small muscles of the body.

While helping young children develop muscle strength, draw attention to the ways their bodies are working when they lift a heavy object. Ask questions that bring attention to which muscles are engaged ("Where do you feel your muscles stretching when you hold this for 10 seconds? What about 30 seconds? Let's count!").

You can combine multiple gross motor skills by attaching heavy objects to a tricycle and encouraging children to peddle vigorously with the added weight. You might say, "How does it feel different when you put this big jug on your handlebars and try and pedal? Let's experiment!" Load heavy rocks or wood chunks into a wagon and invite children to push or pull it across the playground. As children balance on a beam, a row of blocks, or a curb, invite them to carry a heavy object. Encourage them to hold the heavy object with one hand and out to the side to vary their center of gravity.

Tree Cookies

As a child tries to balance, you will usually see a mix of nervousness and concentration in their intense expression. They feel different muscles engaging, a little fear of being off the ground, and excitement when they succeed. You will notice they watch their feet at first, gradually turning their eyes forward as their comfort level increases. The vestibular system, which provides information about the position of the head in space, continues to develop in the early childhood years. The brain sends messages to the body telling it what to do to stay upright (Burgoyne & Ketcham 2015).

Tree cookies are a great natural material children can use to practice their balancing skills. When first introducing tree cookies, choose pieces that are no more than two to three inches thick. Children at the beginning stages of developing balance will have more difficulty staying on small objects, so using pieces that are low to the ground will prevent injuries if children fall. As children's balancing skills improve, you can add thicker pieces that are higher off the ground. Line the tree cookies up with each one about six to 10 inches apart. To increase the challenge, you might include a few pieces farther apart or closer together. To add another level of motivation for children to participate in the activity, ask children questions like "How did you keep your foot on the stump without it falling?" and "How else could we set up the tree cookies?" In contrast to a fixed balance beam, with tree cookies, children can help change the pattern, height, and the distance between their steps.

As you demonstrate how to use the different-size tree cookies, use self-talk to describe what your muscles and different body parts are doing. You can also model falling off an object, letting the children know that it's okay to fall, stand back up, and try again. This goes a long way in fostering children's feelings of success and realization that the more they practice a skill, the better they get at it.

For older preschoolers who are more familiar with balancing, draw attention to their success by saying, "You've gotten so good at balancing on one foot on that tree cookie! What are some other body parts you can balance on?" You may also create nonlinear paths with the tree cookies, creating a zigzag or loop, which increases the level of challenge as children will need to be aware of how the path is changing as they remain balanced.

Balls of Various Sizes and Weights

Many gross motor skills, including hitting or striking, kicking, throwing, catching, and balancing, can be addressed using balls of various weights and sizes. Offer balls made of soft materials like foam or cotton and more rigid materials like plastic or rubber. Encourage children to get to know the properties of the balls they are using, drawing attention to size, texture, weight, and firmness. Ask a child to describe what their legs and arms are doing when they try to kick or throw a ball or to tell you about the shape and texture of the ball. They might call it a circle, presenting you with the opportunity to introduce the word *sphere*.

Children who are in the beginning stages of learning to hit and kick may be nervous or unsure of how to coordinate their bodies in response to a moving ball. Place the ball on a tee or cone to provide stability so children can strike at it with less risk of falling down. Start with large balls (e.g., kickballs, foam soccer balls) so that there is more surface area for children to hit. As children become more comfortable with using stationary balls, increase the challenge by securing the ball to a doorknob for easy kicking. Push a ball through one leg of a pair of sturdy pantyhose and tie the other end to the doorknob to create a tether. Tying a ball next to a wall allows children with less coordination to use the wall for balance as they practice kicking. You might also encourage children to practice striking in a similar way by hanging a balloon from the ceiling or the top of a door frame. Both methods are self-correcting; the child can practice the skill repeatedly without needing to chase the ball, making this an ideal modification for gross motor play indoors.

As children develop greater coordination, introduce smaller balls and encourage children to experiment with their movements. Challenge them to close their eyes, kick the ball, and then describe what happened. You can also ask, "Does it feel different when you kick the ball really hard compared to when you kick it really softly? What happens?"

Throwing and catching are two *very* different skills. Younger children may not be ready to try catching a ball, whereas older preschoolers with more ball experience may show excitement for it. Provide soft balls (e.g., beach balls, foam balls, yarn balls) for younger children to simply toss up and down. Gradually introduce other types of balls, and encourage children to try catching them.

As children's interest in balls fluctuates, continue adding novelty and intrigue. Incorporate new challenges and ways to engage with the balls, asking questions along the way. For example, older preschoolers can practice their aim while throwing by using empty water bottles (with sand or water added to them for weight) as targets to knock down. Depending on what material is used to weight the bottles, children will increase the strength of their throws. Encourage children to help find new ways to use balls or even create an entirely new type of ball ("What kind of target can we make to show you where to aim the ball?," "We got these balls from the store. What materials in the classroom could we use to make our own ball for kicking and throwing?").

Conclusion

Play materials that support children's gross motor development have significant benefits that go beyond just increasing muscle strength and improving coordination. Skills like verbal communication, creative problem solving, and perseverance are all embedded when you intentionally select play materials and scaffold children's learning with these materials. Engaging with gross motor play materials helps children gain confidence and be comfortable with using their bodies *and* minds, and encourages them discover the connection between the two.

TECH TIPS

- Encourage children to use stopwatches to measure and compare how long they and their peers take completing various activities or challenges (e.g., balancing on one foot, carrying heavy objects from one point to another).

- Join a live online exercise class or take advantage of the many movement videos on websites such as GoNoodle.

- Invite children to weigh objects with a digital scale and to make a chart or graph to display and compare the results.

- Using a digital camera, you and the children can take photos of children in different poses as they engage in various gross motor activities. Print and label the photos for display in the classroom or to create a class Body Book.

Suggested Play Materials

Wrist Flexibility

- Hinged boxes to open and close
- Latch boards
- Padlocks and keys
- Paint and painting accessories (e.g., easels, paintbrushes, palettes)
- Shovels
- Trays to carry and balance objects on

Hand Strength

- Building toys to connect and take apart (e.g., bristle blocks, DUPLO blocks, linking cubes, star builders)
- Knob puzzles
- Playdough and clay
- Real tools that require a gripping, flexing, or squeezing motion to use (e.g., binder clips, hole punchers, plastic knives, rolling pins, rubber bands, scissors, spray bottles, tongs, turkey basters)

Finger Dexterity and Precision

- Aluminum foil and items to be wrapped (e.g., figurines, rocks, seashells)
- Beads and string (e.g., floss, shoelaces, yarn)
- Containers with a slit in the lid for items to be slotted into
- Embroidering, sewing, or weaving materials (e.g., embroidery hoops, fabric scraps, looms, plastic sewing needles, thread, yarn)
- Lacing cards
- Nuts and bolts
- Potato Heads
- Real tools that require a pinching motion to use (e.g., clothespins, eye droppers, pipettes, tweezers)
- Stencils and pencils (e.g., golf, standard, thicker width, triangular)

CHAPTER 15

Play Materials That Enhance My Fine Motor Skills

Our hands work every day to help us with tasks that require holding and manipulating objects, from eating to opening containers to turning book pages. Like any other muscle in the body, the small muscles that control these movements need to be exercised. Having a stable base of fine motor skills allows young children to do many things, including caring for their personal needs, such as buttoning or zipping their coats, and participating in literacy activities, such as drawing and writing. To develop these skills, children need a wide range of experiences using the different muscle groups of the wrists, hands, and fingers. Preschoolers are still developing the muscle structures to support the full range of motion in their hands (Huffman & Fortenberry 2011). With time and frequent use, children build up the precision and dexterity of these small muscles.

It is important to provide play materials that support a broad range of abilities and stages of muscle development. As you choose play materials with which children can practice their fine motor skills, consider their experiences at home. Sometimes, something as simple as the utensils families use to eat can affect development.

During self-guided play, preschool teacher Mr. Paz walks to the art center and sees 4-year-old Mina using colored pencils and some textured paper at the table. He takes note of how steady and secure the pencil is in her hand. She holds the pencil with a firm yet delicate grip, moving it smoothly across the page. *Mina has an exceptional amount of fine motor control for a 4-year-old*, Mr. Paz thinks.

At the end of the day, Mr. Paz shares his observation with Mina's mother. "She must have a lot of opportunities at home to draw and work with her hands," he comments.

Mina's mother nods and says, "Our family uses chopsticks to eat every meal. Mina's older brother helped her learn, and she has been using them to pick up her food since she was 2 years old."

Mr. Paz makes a mental note to review the play materials in the manipulatives center and make sure there are options available for children with different levels of ability in using their hands, including Mina's well-developed fine motor skills.

Engaging with fine motor play materials often requires hand–eye coordination, which has been linked to school readiness (University of Leeds 2018). Activities like lacing, buttoning, and cutting stimulate the brain and encourage higher levels of cognitive processing (Grissmer et al. 2010). Knowing the impact of physical development on learning, teachers can provide many play materials that help children develop the different muscle groups. Most children now enter preschool with the ability to point at and swipe a screen (Rideout & Robb 2020). While the isolation of one finger is beneficial, there is conflicting research on the positive and negative effects of touchscreen use. While some studies have shown that children who use touchscreens for more than 60 minutes per week have weaker fine motor skills (Lin, Cherng, & Chen 2017), others have shown that children who use touchscreens have slightly more advanced fine motor skills (Souto et al. 2020).

Padlocks and Keys

Take a moment and think about how your hand moves when opening a lock. This gripping and twisting motion can be unusual for young children who are not usually encouraged to move their hand in this way. A padlock and key provide an experience that has a positive effect on developing wrist strength. Since hand dominance (left-handed or right-handed) is mostly established by age 4 (Johnston et al. 2009), giving the wrist added exercises supports more intensive writing skills.

Introduce a collection of three or four padlocks with keys on individual rings. Padlocks can be placed in a basket with each key ring and children can use trial and error to unlock each lock. As they insert and twist the keys, ask "Can you explain how you are moving your hand to unlock the lock?" Drawing attention to this movement lets children know that you value their developing strength and skill.

To prevent children from becoming bored with padlocks, you might create games that incorporate them. Using easy-peel or erasable stickers, label each lock and key with a color or shape. Children can sort through the locks to find the matching keys. If colors and shapes become too simple, increase the challenge for children by using more complex matching or coding systems (e.g., written numerals on keys and the corresponding number of dots on locks; lowercase letters on keys and uppercase letters on locks). Children will enjoy the novelty of this experience while also practicing their fine motor skills.

Sewing Materials

Similar to lacing cards or stringing beads, the motion of pushing and pulling yarn or thread through a hole is an advanced skill for young children. To introduce the concept of sewing, read a familiar story such as *Corduroy* (by Don Freeman). Before finishing the story, ask the children, "How will Corduroy attach a new button?" Offer children fabric scraps with prepunched holes, burlap, mesh netting, buttons, and yarn or thread. Children whose fine motor skills are in the early stages of development will find it easier to use their fingers at first rather than plastic sewing needles, but have the needles available for them to try and then use more regularly when they're ready.

Playful Problem Solving

Have you ever wondered what would happen if the doll clothes vanished from the dramatic play center? Would the children look to find where they went? What would happen if in their place there appeared fabric scraps with prepunched holes, yarn (or thread), and plastic sewing needles?

Providing these play materials as replacements for doll clothes will not only spark preschoolers' creativity and collaboration skills but also develop their fine motor skills. As children practice their pincer grasp on the needle and lace thread through from hole to hole, they are strengthening the muscles in their fingers and increasing their precision.

As children develop more stability with their grip on the needles, encourage them to sew several pieces of fabric together to create something, such as clothing for a doll. Comment on how they are connecting the pieces of fabric and ask questions that prompt them to think more deeply about the play materials ("Have you ever seen anyone use a needle and thread like this before?," "What else do you think we could make with these sewing materials?").

Nuts and Bolts

Nuts and bolts—whether large, colorful, and plastic or small and metallic—provide children with opportunities for fine motor learning and development. As children screw the nuts onto the bolts using their fingers or a wrench, they engage in motions that stretch and strengthen the muscles of the wrist and develop the ability to flex their fingers. Additionally, the complex act of turning an object with one hand while using the other hand to hold a different object in place requires a coordination of skills and mental processes.

Younger preschoolers may begin exploring this play material before they can fully manipulate it by raking through a bin of plastic nuts and bolts and opening and closing their hand around them. Children may also attempt to fit the nuts and bolts together as they investigate the thread (that is, the spiral-ridged end of the bolt onto which nuts are twisted) on each piece. Support children at this stage by pointing out the threaded sections ("I see these little lines and grooves; I wonder what they are for"). Teachers may also notice that children try to put the nuts and bolts together by inserting and pushing on one end. Give children plenty of exploration time to discover if their solution works or not. If their trial and error results in frustration before they try other ways of making the nut and bolt fit together, you might ask them why they think the pieces are not connecting easily and help them come up with alternate solutions to try.

As older preschoolers gain control and precision over their hand movements, introduce real nuts and bolts. A woodworking center or makerspace is an ideal place to support children at this level as they engage in an engineering design or woodworking project where they have to link objects together. Discuss how the bolts can be used to connect various materials.

Conclusion

As children's fine motor skills increase over time, continue to challenge them by adding play materials that are more complex or require more refined precision and strength for children to succeed. Support children at all levels of fine motor development by observing them at play and crafting experiences that strengthen the developing muscles in their wrists, hands, and fingers.

TECH TIPS

- Search online with children for projects to build with LEGO bricks and encourage them to recreate them.

- Introduce a digital dynamometer, a device that measures force. Invite children to use the dynamometer to measure their handgrip strength, record the results, and compare them with those of their peers.

- Download game apps, such as the Scriba Snap, that require use of a stylus and respond to pressure.

- Cut a finger off an old glove for children to wear while using touchscreen devices, such as tablets. This helps children have an easier time focusing on using just one finger on the touchscreen.

Suggested Play Materials

Awareness of Body Parts

- Games that require coordination and kinesthetic awareness (e.g., Jump the River, limbo, Spiderwebs)
- Human figures with poseable body parts
- Mirrors, both full length and handheld
- Songs that identify body parts (e.g., "Head, Shoulders, Knees, and Toes," "The Hokey Pokey," "La Tía Mónica")
- X-rays of the human body
- Yoga mats and books and cards with yoga poses

Healthy Eating

- Cooking appliances, both pretend and real that are nonfunctioning and with cords removed (e.g., chapati press, moka pot, toaster oven)
- Play foods from a wide variety of cultures
- Portion plates
- Recipe books and cards
- Serving bowls and platters for family-style dining

Self-Help, Self-Care, and Hygiene

- Child-size serving utensils and drinkware (e.g., pitchers, spoons, tongs)
- Dressing boards
- Dress-up clothing and accessories for doctor or hospital dramatic play (e.g., physician bags, scrubs, stethoscopes, tongue depressors)
- Dress-up clothing and doll clothing with fasteners (e.g., buttons, laces, snaps, Velcro, zippers)
- Lacing cards
- Posters outlining steps of routines (e.g., brushing hair, brushing teeth, handwashing)
- Timers for brushing teeth and washing hands
- Toothbrushes and model teeth

CHAPTER 16

Play Materials That Help Me Understand My Body

As a young child's body grows and develops, so should their understanding of how it works. Preschoolers continue to learn how their bodies move and what their bodies are capable of as they progress out of their toddler years. They become more adept at controlling their basic body movements as they prepare to head into kindergarten (Ozmun & Gallahue 2017). By engaging with play materials that promote awareness of different body parts and that help develop coordination, balance, and strong muscles, children experience the workings of their bodies in meaningful contexts. However, understanding the relationship between using these play materials and how they impact the body requires more thoughtful input from teachers. To help extend children's learning about the systems of the body, incorporate questions and comments that inspire children to think more deeply about their body movements ("What are your arms doing while you're balancing on one foot?," "What happens to your balance when your arms are above your head instead of stretched out on either side of your body?").

Consistent personal care routines throughout the preschool years also set children up for increased success as they transition into the more rigorous daily routines and expectations of elementary school. These health and wellness routines help children learn how to care for their bodies and include everything from eating healthy and staying clean to buttoning their own coat and tying their shoes. At first, children's understanding of these concepts will largely depend on their routines at home. Be patient and consistent. To help children develop strong healthy habits, embed play materials that promote daily hygiene and self-care routines in your early learning setting.

When young children ask you questions about their bodies, answer them honestly. Body curiosity is a natural part of preschoolers' developmental progression, and children should not be shamed for their inquisitiveness or desire to understand. If you are unsure of the right things to say, consult with your program's nurse and with families to decide on the best approach.

Games That Require Coordination and Kinesthetic Awareness

Games that require children to use and coordinate their bodies help them build awareness of their bodies and what they can do, promote overall physical health and development, and are fun. Introduce children to the concept of navigating their bodies through space by first engaging them in a game of limbo or Jump the River. In limbo, a stick or rope is held above the child's head for them to pass under while bending backward; the stick is gradually lowered as the game goes on. In Jump the River, children step or hop over a rope that begins on the ground and is raised higher as the game progresses. During gameplay, introduce positional words like *over, under, higher*, and *lower*.

Spiderwebs is a game that combines the movements and skills needed for both limbo and Jump the River. An obstacle course is created by weaving string through and around various sturdy objects. Indoors, this can include doorknobs and furniture legs; outdoors, consider fences, light poles, and trees. The aim of the game is for children to navigate their way through the spiderwebs without touching or getting tangled up in crisscrossed strings. To accomplish this, children experiment with ways to bend and twist their bodies.

For younger preschoolers or children with physical delays, use crepe paper streamers that will easily break when a child gets a foot or hand caught in it. As they become familiar with the activity and how their bodies move in space, you might try a more rigid material like yarn and or twine. Vary the height, length, and angle of the spiderwebs to provide visual interest and challenge. You can begin by building the spiderwebs yourself, but inviting the children to help as their experience with this game grows is an excellent way to encourage collaboration and teamwork.

Encourage children to pay attention to how their bodies move through each level of string and what each body part needs to do to stay balanced. While children engage with this play material, ask questions like the following to support the executive function skills responsible for planning, adaptable thinking, and persistence:

> "What is your plan for getting through the spiderwebs?"

> "Is this string lower or higher than your belly button?"

> "You made it all the way to the other side! What's the first (next, last) thing you did when you started moving across?"

> "What do you think you need to do with your head and chest to get under this very low spiderweb? Is there any other way you could get through it?"

> "Hakim has a hard time getting through this spiderweb because of his wheelchair. Can you and Gianna design a new spiderweb that Hakim can get through with his chair? How will you do it?"

Spiderwebs can be set up as part of indoor gross motor time. If space allows, leave it in intact; if not, you can break it down each time after the activity is completed. The spiderwebs can be simple or complex, depending on the available space and the developmental abilities of the children you teach.

Child-Size Serving Utensils and Drinkware

Incorporating child-size serving utensils and drinkware into mealtimes gives preschoolers the chance to practice fine motor, self-regulation, and self-help skills; enjoy feelings of increased independence and autonomy; and learn how their bodies move when manipulating objects (Waldron 2020). If your program does not implement family-style dining (when food is placed in the center of the table at group mealtimes and children use small utensils to serve themselves), consider including at least a few opportunities for children to serve their own food and drinks. You might have child-size pitchers available for pouring milk or water into cups, plastic knives for cutting up bananas, or small tongs for picking up bread and cheese cubes.

Children's comfort level with this practice will again depend on their experiences at home or in previous early learning settings. Give children ample time to practice these skills before expecting them to be proficient at it. When first introducing serving utensils and drinkware into mealtimes, expect some messes. Children who are new to this practice may overfill a cup or use two hands to hold tongs. Begin by offering hand-over-hand support, placing your hand gently over the child's to help keep the utensil steady and guide movement. Over time and with practice, children will be able to perform these tasks more independently. The process of learning how much pressure is needed to squeeze tongs, how to angle their hand while scooping, and when to stop pouring is complicated for a preschooler! They are only just beginning to understand how their bodies move and work.

As children get comfortable with serving themselves and coordinating muscle groups, this part of the daily routine may take a little longer than expected. Again, patience and consistency give children a safe, predictable atmosphere for developing these very important self-help skills.

Make sure to acknowledge and celebrate when children successfully use these materials ("You poured the water into the cup and stopped before it reached the top," "You were able to bring that spoon all the way from the big bowl to your plate without spilling any fruit on the table!").

Dress-Up Clothing and Doll Clothing with Fasteners

As children gain self-regulation skills and working memory, they move from needing help to perform self-care tasks to doing them independently. Fine motor development plays a role in this process, as children are able to snap and Velcro (a process that requires fitting together and pulling apart elements) before they can zipper and button (a process that requires precise actions with opposing hand movements) (Epstein, Marshall, & Gainsley 2016). Part of this progression also involves understanding how the body moves. As children learn to dress themselves, they use different muscle groups—raising their arms, bending their elbows, lifting their legs. Giving children experiences to practice moving their bodies in these ways helps them to discover more about what their bodies can do.

Children of all abilities must be considered when deciding what kind of dressing materials to include in your early learning setting. For example, children with limited fine motor skills or vision impairment will have an easier time with Velcro than with small buttons (Brillante 2017). When choosing dress-up clothing for the dramatic play center, pay close attention to how each article of clothing fastens. Are there opportunities for children to snap, Velcro,

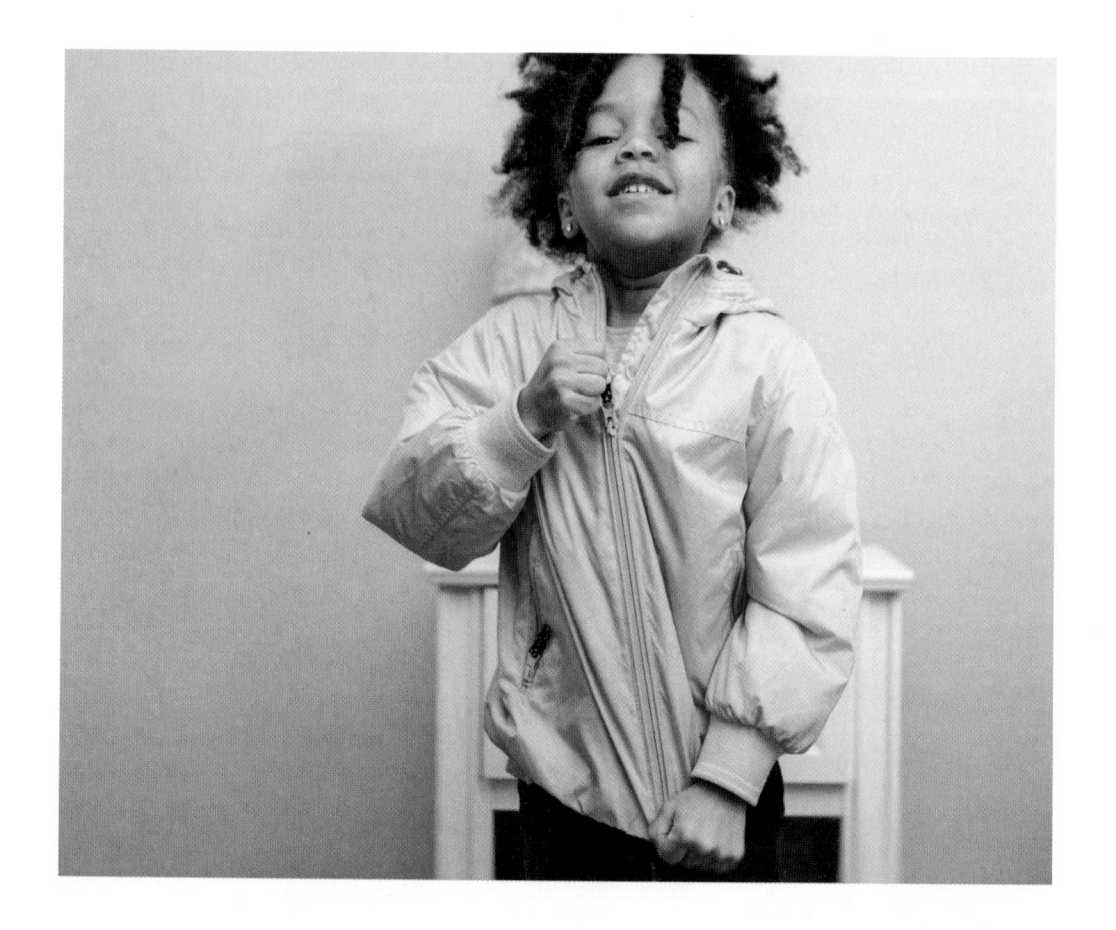

button, zipper, and tie? Do children understand the purpose of these fasteners and what happens when they are not fastened properly? Extend children's understanding of this concept by asking questions like these:

> "How are these two kinds of fasteners different (the same)?"

> "Which shirt is easiest for you to put on? Why do you think that is?"

> "Can you describe what you are doing with your arm to fit into that jacket?"

> "What might happen if you don't close up the jacket all the way?"

Some children might be uncomfortable using dress-up clothes on their own bodies and may find more comfort in dressing dolls. While children are dressing dolls in the dramatic play center, help them make the connection to experiences with their own clothing. Draw attention to how they lift a doll's arms or legs and how that relates to their own movements when dressing.

Conclusion

Learning how the body works and how to care for oneself during the preschool years is a process. Incorporate play materials and experiences into your early learning setting and its daily routines that help young children gain confidence in their ability to do things for themselves.

TECH TIPS

- Use a camera or smartphone with a slow-motion feature to record children engaged in a gross motor movement (e.g., Hula-Hooping, jumping, running) or a self-care routine. Watch the recording together and point out different parts of the body as they move. Ask questions that prompt children to think more deeply about their bodies ("What do you notice about your arms while you're running?," "Did you notice how this arm goes forward when this foot goes back?").

- Search online with children for information on healthy foods and yoga poses to incorporate into the learning environment and activities.

- Use a mini-blender to help children make healthy snacks, like fruit smoothies.

- Use hands-free soap dispensers, hand dryers, or faucets when possible. This not only reduces cross-contamination but also gives children an opportunity to explore and discuss what makes these machines work.

- Incorporate digital and analog timers while children are washing their hands or brushing their teeth. This opens the door to discussions about why it is important to engage in some hygiene routines for a certain amount of time. You can also integrate math learning by drawing attention to the numbers on the timer.

Suggested Play Materials

Sound

- Musical instruments with different tones (e.g., guitars, harmonicas, pianos or keyboards, xylophones)
- Musical shakers, both store bought (e.g., egg shakers, maracas, rainsticks, rattles) and those made with found, recyclable, and natural materials
- Tone blocks

Sight

- Color paddles and wheels
- Flashlights
- Gyroscopes
- Kaleidoscopes
- Memory or scavenger hunt games (e.g., *I Spy* books or board games, small items hidden in playdough or sand)
- Pattern cards
- Prisms

Touch

- Fabrics with different textures
- Finger paints
- Flooring samples (e.g., carpeting, concrete, cork, glazed or terracotta tiles, hardwood, linoleum, rubber, stone, turf, vinyl)
- Sand
- Sandpaper of various grits
- Water

Taste

- Food charts where children can identify sweet, salty, sour, and bitter
- Foods from various cultures
- Fresh fruits from around the world

Smell

- Matching games using tea bags and scented oils
- Natural items with strong scents (e.g., cedar wood, lavender, mint, oregano, pine needles)
- Scent bottles
- Scented art materials (e.g., markers, paint, playdough)

CHAPTER 17

Play Materials That Stimulate My Senses

Preschoolers use their senses to interpret and make meaning of the world around them. They seek out and enjoy experiences that encourage them to learn through smell, touch, sight, taste, and sound. Think about a young child who pets a cat or dog. They might smile and laugh, the physical sensation of touching fur sending a message to their brain and letting them know it feels good to pet something soft. In moments like this, the senses are a language for how children learn and a lens through which they can explore how their body processes information.

Children sometimes have difficulty expressing what they are experiencing because they are limited by vocabulary. They have not yet developed the cognitive processes to always make sense of what certain sensations are telling them (NAEYC 2022). Teachers help children understand these sensory experiences and provide language children can use to communicate about them. You can also encourage children to practice using senses they are less familiar with.

> The children in Ms. Lang's preschool learning setting hear the beeping of a truck backing up.
>
> Bethany jumps up and says, "I hear a truck."
>
> The windows are covered, so Ms. Lang asks her, "How did you know it was a truck?"
>
> "I heard it," responds Bethany.
>
> The next day at whole group time, Ms. Lang takes out the tablet and wireless speaker. She plays a variety of sounds and encourages the children to identify what they think is making that sound without looking at the tablet screen. The sounds are a combination of everyday objects being shaken or tapped, animal noises, and weather events. Often, Ms. Lang has to play the sounds more than once for the children to identify them, but she realizes the value in this experience: children are practicing relying on their sense of hearing and making connections between new and familiar sounds.

Once children have had plenty of experiences exploring their senses with concrete play materials, they will be better equipped to interact with and understand their environment.

Musical Shakers

Musical shakers come in many varieties—think of maracas, rainsticks, and the egg shakers that come with many commercial instrument sets. Because of their shape, size, and contents, each of these objects produces a variety of sounds. Encourage children to experiment with the shakers and listen for the different effects.

Children can also create their own musical shakers using found, recyclable, and natural play materials. For containers, provide materials that are sturdy and that will create different sounds when filled. These might include small milk cartons, cookie tins, empty water bottles, yogurt cups, and CD cases. Offer children a wide range of materials to fill these containers, including sand, marker caps, pebbles, bolts, rubber washers, and beads. With the help of an adult, have children securely seal these containers with strong tape, contact paper, or glue.

Encourage children to listen to and compare how the different materials inside the shaker sound when combined with the different containers. Play listening games with children, inviting them to identify what play material is inside the shaker. As children become familiar with the sounds, encourage them to combine two or more materials inside the shakers for a more challenging identification.

Sand

Sand, with its smooth texture and cold temperature, is a soothing play material for children who need extra sensory input to stay calm and focused. Early childhood teachers will often find a child who needs a break from an active learning setting quietly running their hands through the contents of the sand table. Spending 10 to 15 minutes at the sand table, alone or with a peer, can calm a child down who is having difficulty regulating their emotions.

Provide sand for sensory play in durable containers with approximately six inches of sand, enough to easily scoop and pour. Add a few drops of scented oil to the sand so the smell wafts up as children move the sand around. You might also place small objects in the sand for children to discover as they dig with spoons and shovels. This scavenger hunt-type experience also supports visual processing. Other similar materials, such as birdseed, potting soil, or magnetic sand, can be substituted in for new sensory play experiences throughout the school year; however, avoid using food items like rice, pasta, or dried beans. Families have different relationships with and access to food, and it should not be provided as a play material.

Children's enjoyment of filling containers and then dumping their contents is most common in toddlerhood, but that interest carries over into the early preschool years and even beyond for some children. A sand table offers an appropriate alternative for children who express this interest by dumping bins of toys around the learning setting. You can redirect this kind of behavior with comments like "Dumping these bins of toys in the block center makes a

mess and is not okay, but we can go over to the sand table and dump some buckets of sand!" Children practice hand–eye coordination and explore cause and effect while they fill and dump in the sand table (McMullen & Brody 2022).

As children engage in sand play both indoors and out, introduce rich vocabulary that is tied to their senses, such as the following:

> *Smooth, squishy, grainy, cool, rough* (touch)

> *Scented, aromatic, earthy* (smell)

> *Whispery, scratchy* (sound)

> *Grainy, depth, buried, multicolored* (sight)

Scent Bottles

Smell is one of young children's most powerful senses. It is how infants distinguish between unfamiliar adults, know when their mother is close, and determine whether they are safe (Schaal et al. 2020). By isolating children's sense of smell, you help them to actively participate in processing information. Scent bottles are a great way to explore this sense.

To create scent bottles, place cotton balls soaked in various extracts into small plastic salt and pepper shakers. Extracts come in a wide variety of scents, from fruits and spices to florals and herbs. Place the scent bottles on a table in the science center and invite children to investigate. Begin with two or three of the most recognizable scents, such as vanilla, mint, and orange. Ask "Can you describe what that bottle smells like?" or "Where have you smelled that before?" Encourage children to use their sense of smell to identify different scents or even share how a certain scent makes them feel. Listen to the stories that some of the scents evoke in children's memories. Children may talk about scents based on where they have experienced them. For example, a child might say the mint bottle smells like gum, which provides an opportunity to extend children's understanding of how things are made.

After children have had some experience with familiar scents, add bottles with scents that children may be less familiar with. Try lemon, almond, maple, or anise. If they have difficulty identifying the scent when putting their nose up to the bottle, wave it back and forth to lessen the intensity. Barring any allergies and your program's policies, you might also bring in foods flavored like one of these unfamiliar scents so that children can experience it in a different way.

Another option is to move from extracts to essential oils. Oils can be more nuanced in their odors and make for a more challenging identification. As children discover scents they like, consider adding a few drops into a playdough recipe or even to your water table.

Another way to encourage children to experience the world through their senses is to experiment with taking one of those senses away. For example, discovery bags invite children to use all of their senses except sight to identify a hidden object. Place a familiar play material, such as a small car, play food, or a crayon, into an opaque bag. Pass the bag around to each child and encourage them to try identifying the object by reaching inside to feel it without looking. Talk with them about shape, texture, and size as well as the smell and sound, asking questions or making comments:

- "Tell me how the material feels in your hand."

- "Put your nose in the top of the bag, but don't look at what's inside! Tell us what you smell."

- "What do you hear when you shake the bag around?"

After identifying the play material for themselves, older preschoolers might enjoy the added challenge of describing the object to other children to see if they can guess what it is based on their descriptions.

Conclusion

Young children digest valuable information about their world through their senses. For preschoolers, a combination of experiences and hands-on activities with carefully selected play materials that isolate or call attention to those senses promotes their ability to construct knowledge and make sense of the vast amount of learning taking place in the early learning setting.

TECH TIPS

- Search online for animal and environmental sounds. Play them and encourage children to identify them.

- Have children record their voices and then play them back to try and identify whose voice it is. Use voice changer apps for children to experiment with pitch and sound effects.

- Search online with children for Braille writing and American Sign Language (ASL) gestures. Label several play materials in the classroom with Braille and/or a picture of the ASL hand, arm, and body gestures (Brillante 2017).

- Use an overhead projector or flashlight to create shadow stories. Ask children to hold up play materials, props, or just their hands in front of the light to act out story scenes from a book or ones they make up.

- Use an aromatherapy diffuser and essential oils to scent the classroom.

Summary and Reflection

In addition to helping children build and refine their gross and fine motor skills, scaffolding children's physical learning and development promotes healthy lifestyle choices and calls attention to movement as an authentic language for self-expression. The play materials you provide encourage children to develop a wide "vocabulary" of movements. As children learn more about what their bodies are capable of and how they work, take advantage of the many teachable moments that occur by making comments and asking questions that make them think more deeply. Draw connections between eating habits and self-care routines children experience in the early learning setting and at home. Consider how to incorporate gross motor experiences indoors. Think about how and when to incorporate sensory experiences. Above all, give children the space to play.

Now Ask Yourself This

- Do you have any interests that involve health and wellness (e.g., healthy cooking, favorite exercise routines)?

- Do you see yourself as a physically active person? How does that shape the play materials and experiences you include in your early learning setting?

- How do you respond when you find something physically challenging?

- How do you support children through moments when they experience a physical limitation?

- How do you respond when children express curiosity about their own body parts?

Final Thoughts

Each play material in your early learning setting offers a different opportunity for children to learn and communicate what they already know. Children are diverse learners and express their knowledge in various ways. An early learning environment that supports multimodal learning through a wide variety of play materials opens the door for young children to construct and express knowledge using one or more of their hundred languages (Rumenapp, Morales, & Lykouretzos 2018).

As you explore the play materials and suggestions in this book, remember that preschoolers' learning and development is on a spectrum, and they progress and develop different skills at different rates. You and children's families know the children best. Be mindful of children who need a bit of an extra challenge as well as those who may not be developmentally ready for the materials or activities you present. The variety of play materials and the thoughtfulness of your interactions will guide children's growth and development.

You are a creative professional. The ways you expand and develop your teaching style is an expression of creativity and individuality. You bring unique strengths to your early learning community and the children you work with. You make the materials come to life. Even the act of reading this book says much about your commitment to young children and the vast field of early childhood education.

To those of you who have a deep connection to play and who thrive on the excitement of discovering—or rediscovering—the special things about the children you work with, thank you for going on this journey, for being open to thinking about play materials in different and unique ways, and for opening your minds to the exciting process of choosing the right stuff.

Appendix A

Highlights of Learning, Development, and Positive Well-Being

Preschoolers (3 to 5 Years)

Cognitive Learning, Development, and Well-Being

I learn how to integrate new knowledge and problem solve.

I scribble and draw people-like figures.

I say or sing letters.

I name numbers and rote count.

I understand simple positional words.

I repeat rhymes, make up alliterative phrases, and isolate syllables.

I like to make and count collections of objects.

I speak in short sentences.

I use pronouns when I talk about others.

I understand similarities and differences.

I make predictions about what will happen when someone is reading a book to me.

I remember details from a story.

I identify, explore, and create patterns.

Social and Emotional Learning, Development, and Well-Being

I learn how to take care of myself, express how I feel, and relate to others.

I express my emotions, learn to name them, and practice controlling them.

I learn to share.

I show concern for others.

I like to act out family roles.

I like to play with other children.

I dress and undress myself.

I want to play with my teachers.

I understand and follow simple directions.

I use my imagination to play pretend.

I understand that we can feel different about the same thing.

I show more desire to be independent.

I label my peers as friends.

Physical Learning, Development, and Well-Being

I learn how my body works.

I walk and run around objects.

I can stand on one foot for five seconds.

I climb ladders.

I march.

I use alternating feet to go up or down the stairs.

I use scissors with control.

I can catch a bounced ball.

I hop on one foot.

I skip.

I hit or kick balls.

I bend over to pick up something without falling.

I hold pencils and crayons between my fingers and thumb.

I string items like beads together.

Adapted from and informed by CDC (n.d. b, c, d) and HealthyChildren.org (n.d.)

Appendix B

On the Bookshelf

Support My Language and Literacy Skills

- *Jamberry*, by Bruce Degen

- *The Napping House*, by Audrey Wood, illustrated by Don Wood

- *P Is for Poppadoms! An Indian Alphabet Book*, by Kabir Sehgal and Surishtha Sehgal, illustrated by Hazel Ito

- *Snip Snap! What's That?* by Mara Bergman, illustrated by Nick Maland

- *Z Is for Moose*, by Kelly Bingham, illustrated by Paul O. Zelinsky

Teach Me Mathematical Concepts

- *Ants Rule: The Long and Short of It*, by Bob Barner

- *Baby Goes to Market*, by Atinuke, illustrated by Angela Brooksbank

- *The Carpenter*, by Bruna Barros

- *I Know Numbers!* by Taro Gomi

- *Just How Long Can a Long String Be?!* by Keith Baker

- *Round Is a Tortilla: A Book of Shapes*, by Roseanne Greenfield Thong, illustrated by John Parra

Encourage Me to Build and Engineer

- *Changes, Changes*, by Pat Hutchins

- *Dreaming Up: A Celebration of Building*, by Christy Hale

- *Houses and Homes*, by Ann Morris, photographs by Ken Heyman

- *How a House Is Built*, by Gail Gibbons

- *If I Built a House*, by Chris Van Dusen

- *If You Lived Here: Houses of the World*, by Giles Laroche

- *The Most Magnificent Thing*, by Ashley Spires

- *Roll, Slope, and Slide: A Book About Ramps*, by Michael Dahl, illustrated by Denise Shea

- *When I Build with Blocks*, by Niki Alling

Inspire Scientific Inquiry and Innovation

- *Ada Twist, Scientist*, by Andrea Beaty, illustrated by David Roberts

- *Going Places*, by Peter Reynolds and Paul Reynolds

- *How Do You Lift a Lion?* by Robert E. Wells

- *I Use Science Tools*, by Kelli Hicks

- *If I Built a Car*, by Chris Van Dusen

- *Not a Box*, by Antoinette Portis

- *Pull, Lift, and Lower: A Book About Pulleys*, by Michael Dahl, illustrated by Denise Shea

- *Ten Seeds*, by Ruth Brown

- *Up, Down, and Around*, by Katherine Ayres, illustrated by Nadine Bernard Westcott

- *What Does the X-Ray Say?* by the Second Grade Students of Longfellow Elementary in West Allis, Wisconsin

Help Me Understand Nature

- *Before We Eat: From Farm to Table*, by Pat Brisson, illustrated by Mary Azarian

- *Creature Features: Twenty-Five Animals Explain Why They Look the Way They Do*, by Steve Jenkins and Robin Page

- *The Home Builders*, by Varsha Bajaj, illustrated by Simona Mulazzani

- *Playing with Lanterns*, by Wang Yage, illustrated by Zhu Chengliang

- *Pumpkin Jack*, by Will Hubbell

- *Sweater Weather*, by Matt Phelan

- *What Do You Do with a Tail Like This?* by Steve Jenkins and Robin Page

Part Three: Social and Emotional Learning and Development (Chapters 10–13)

Support My Emotional Intelligence, Relationship Building, and Cooperation Skills

- *Same, Same But Different*, by Jenny Sue Kostecki-Shaw
- *Sometimes I'm Bombaloo*, by Rachel Vail, illustrated by Yumi Heo
- *The Way I Feel*, by Janan Cain
- *What I Like About Me!* by Allia Zobel Nolan, illustrated by Miki Sakamoto
- *Who Are You? The Kid's Guide to Gender Identity*, by Brook Pessin-Whedbee, illustrated by Naomi Bardoff

Invite My Creative Expression Through Visual Arts

- *Anno's Journey*, by Mitsumasa Anno
- *Beautiful Oops!* by Barney Saltzberg
- *A Boy Named Isamu: A Story of Isamu Noguchi*, by James Yang
- *Diego*, by Jonah Winter, illustrated by Jeanette Winter
- *Henri's Scissors*, by Jeanette Winter
- *I Ain't Gonna Paint No More!* by Karen Beaumont, illustrated by David Catrow
- *Joseph Had a Little Overcoat*, by Simms Taback
- *Mix It Up!* by Hervé Tullet
- *The Noisy Paint Box: The Colors and Sounds of Kandinsky's Abstract Art*, by Barb Rosenstock, illustrated by Mary GrandPré
- *Opposites Abstract*, by Mo Willems
- *Pantone: Colors*, by Pantone
- *Pink Is for Boys*, by Robb Pearlman, illustrated by Eda Kaban
- *Tar Beach*, by Faith Ringgold

Encourage Me to Explore and Make Music

- *88 Instruments*, by Chris Barton, illustrated by Louis Thomas
- *The African Orchestra*, by Wendy Hartmann, illustrated by Joan Rankin
- *Because*, by Mo Willems, illustrated by Amber Ren
- *Dancing with Daddy*, by Anitra Rowe Schulte, illustrated by Ziyue Chen
- *Music Everywhere*, by Maya Ajmera, Elise Hofer Derstine, and Cynthia Pon
- *Music Is . . .* by Brandon Stosuy, illustrated by Amy Martin

Inspire Pretend Play and Dramatic Play

- *The Big Umbrella*, by Amy June Bates and Juniper Bates
- *Clothesline Clues to Jobs People Do*, by Kathryn Heling and Deborah Hembrook, illustrated by Andy Robert Davies
- *The Family Book*, by Todd Parr
- *Hats, Hats, Hats*, by Ann Morris, photographs by Ken Heyman
- *¡Hola! Jalapeño*, by Amy Wilson Sanger
- *Julián Is a Mermaid*, by Jessica Love
- *Pancakes! An Interactive Recipe Book*, illustrated by Lotta Nieminen
- *Pretend Soup and Other Real Recipes*, by Mollie Katzen and Ann Henderson
- *Tortillas and Lullabies/Tortillas y cancioncitas*, by Lynn Reiser, illustrated by Corazones Valientes
- *What to Do with a Box*, by Jane Yolen, illustrated by Chris Sheban

Part Four: Physical Learning and Development (Chapters 14–17)

Build My Gross Motor Skills

- *Balancing Act*, by Ellen Stoll Walsh

- *From Head to Toe*, by Eric Carle

- *Move!* by Steve Jenkins and Robin Page

- *Plants Can't Sit Still*, by Rebecca E. Hirsch, illustrated by Mia Posada

- *We All Play*, by Julie Flett

- *You Are a Lion! And Other Fun Yoga Poses*, by Taeeun Yoo

Enhance My Fine Motor Skills

- *Extra Yarn*, by Mac Barnett, illustrated by Jon Klassen

- *Fly Flies*, by Ziggy Hanaor, illustrated by Alice Bowsher

- *Lady Hahn and Her Seven Friends*, by Yumi Heo

- *Perfect Square*, by Michael Hall

- *The Quilt*, by Ann Jonas

- *A Sari for Ammi*, by Mamta Nainy, illustrated by Sandhya Prabhat

Help Me Understand My Body

- *Bend and Stretch: Learning About Your Bones and Muscles*, by Pamela Hill Nettleton, illustrated by Becky Shipe

- *The Boy Who Loved Broccoli*, by Sarah A. Creighton, illustrated by Gene L. Hamilton

- *Eyes That Kiss in the Corners*, by Joanna Ho, illustrated by Dung Ho

- *Good Thing You're Not an Octopus!* by Julie Markes, illustrated by Maggie Smith

- *I Like Myself!* by Karen Beaumont, illustrated by David Catrow

- *We're All Wonders*, by R.J. Palacio

Stimulate My Senses

- *Duck! Rabbit!* by Amy Krouse Rosenthal and Tom Lichtenheld

- *Gregory, the Terrible Eater*, by Mitchell Sharmat, illustrated by Jose Aruego and Ariane Dewey

- *I Feel a Foot!* by Maranke Rinck, illustrated by Martijn van der Linden

- *My Five Senses*, by Aliki

- *Too Much Noise*, by Ann McGovern, illustrated by Simms Taback

References

AR DDCECE (Arkansas Department of Human Services, Division of Child Care and Early Childhood Education) & ARHSSCO (Arkansas Head Start State Collaboration Office). 2016. "Arkansas Child Development and Early Learning Standards: Birth Through 60 Months." Little Rock, AR: AR DDCECE. https://humanservices.arkansas.gov/wp-content/uploads/AR-Early-Learning-Standards-2016-1.pdf.

Auerbach, S. 2012. "Why This Toy?" *NAEYC*. www.naeyc.org/our-work/families/why-this-toy.

Bidzan-Bluma, I., & M. Lipowska. 2018. "Physical Activity and Cognitive Functioning of Children: A Systematic Review." *International Journal of Environmental Research and Public Health* 15 (4): 800. doi:10.3390/ijerph15040800.

Brillante, P. 2017. *The Essentials: Supporting Young Children with Disabilities in the Classroom*. Washington, DC: NAEYC.

Brillante, P. 2018. Reply to "July Book Club: Big Questions for Young Minds: Extending Children's Thinking by Janis Strasser and Lisa Mufson Bresson." *Hello*, July 18. https://hello.naeyc.org/communities/community-home/digestviewer/viewthread?MessageKey=311359a3-0ce8-4663-bfdb-961dff4b9133&CommunityKey=f51f9fd4-47c9-4bfd-aca7-23e9f31b601e&tab=digestviewer#bm311359a3-0ce8-4663-bfdb-961dff4b9133#bm26.

Burgoyne, M.E., & C.J. Ketcham. 2015. "Observation of Classroom Performance Using Therapy Balls as a Substitute for Chairs in Elementary School Children." *Journal of Education and Training Studies* 3 (4): 42–48.

CDC (Centers for Disease Control and Prevention). n.d. a. "CDC Healthy Schools." Last modified December 1, 2021. www.cdc.gov/healthyschools/index.htm.

CDC (Centers for Disease Control and Prevention). n.d. b. "Important Milestones: Your Child By Three Years." Last modified February 7, 2022. www.cdc.gov/ncbddd/actearly/milestones/milestones-3yr.html.

CDC (Centers for Disease Control and Prevention). n.d. c. "Important Milestones: Your Child By Four Years." Last modified February 7, 2022. www.cdc.gov/ncbddd/actearly/milestones/milestones-4yr.html.

CDC (Centers for Disease Control and Prevention). n.d. d. "Important Milestones: Your Child By Five Years." Last modified February 7, 2022. www.cdc.gov/ncbddd/actearly/milestones/milestones-5yr.html.

CPSC (US Consumer Product Safety Commission). n.d. "For Kids' Sake: Think Toy Safety." Publication 281. Accessed February 2, 2022. Bethesda, MD: CPSC. www.cpsc.gov/s3fs-public/pdfs/blk_pdf_281.pdf.

Craft, D.H., & C.L. Smith. 2010. *Active Play! Fun Physical Activities for Young Children*. Cortland, NY: Active Play Books.

DeVries, R., & C. Sales. 2010. *Ramps and Pathways: A Constructivist Approach to Physics with Young Children*. Washington, DC: NAEYC.

de Waal, E. 2019. "Fundamental Movement Skills and Academic Performance of 5- to 6-Year-Old Preschoolers." *Early Childhood Education Journal* 47 (4): 455–64.

Eartheasy. n.d. "Gardening with Children." Accessed February 2, 2022. https://learn.eartheasy.com/guides/gardening-with-children.

Edwards, C., L. Gandini, & G. Forman, eds. 1998. *The Hundred Languages of Children: The Reggio Emilia Approach—Advanced Reflections*. 2nd ed. Greenwich, CT: Ablex.

Eerola, T., A. Friberg, & R. Bresin. 2013. "Emotional Expression in Music: Contribution, Linearity, and Additivity of Primary Musical Cues." *Frontiers in Psychology* 4: 487. doi:10.3389/fpsyg.2013.00487.

Epstein, A.S., B. Marshall, & S. Gainsley. 2016. *COR Advantage Scoring Guide*. Ypsilanti, MI: HighScope Press.

Fantozzi, V.B. 2022. *Digital Tools for Learning, Creating, and Thinking: Developmentally Appropriate Strategies for Early Childhood Educators*. Washington, DC: NAEYC.

Fox, D., & L. Liu. 2012. "Building Musical Bridges: Early Childhood Learning and Musical Play." *Min-Ad: Israel Studies in Musicology Online* 10: 57–67.

Georgia Department of Early Care and Learning. n.d. "The Georgia Early Learning and Development Standards (GELDS)." Accessed February 2, 2022. http://gelds.decal.ga.gov.

Goodway, J.D., J.C. Ozmun, & D.L. Gallahue. 2019. *Understanding Motor Development: Infants, Children, Adolescents, Adults*. 8th ed. Burlington, MA: Jones & Bartlett Learning.

Gosso, Y., & A.M. Almeida Carvalho. 2013. "Play and Cultural Context." In *Encyclopedia on Early Childhood Development: Play*, ed. P.K. Smith. www.child-encyclopedia.com/play /according-experts/play-and-cultural-context.

Grissmer, D., K.J. Grimm, S.M. Aiyer, W.M. Murrah, & J.S. Steele. 2010. "Fine Motor Skills and Early Comprehension of the World: Two New School Readiness Indicators." *Developmental Psychology* 46 (5): 1008–17.

Hansel, R.R. 2016. *Creative Block Play: A Comprehensive Guide to Learning Through Building*. St. Paul, MN: Redleaf Press.

Harms, T., R.M. Clifford, & D. Cryer. 2014. *Early Childhood Environment Rating Scale*. 3rd ed. New York: Teachers College Press.

Hashmi, S., R.E. Vanderwert, A.L. Paine, & S.A. Gerson. 2021. "Doll Play Prompts Social Thinking and Social Talking: Representations of Internal State Language in the Brain." *Developmental Science* e13163. doi:10.1111/desc.13163.

HealthyChildren.org. n.d. "Preschool." Accessed February 2, 2022. https://healthychildren .org/english/ages-stages/preschool/pages/default.aspx.

Heroman, C. 2017. *Making and Tinkering with STEM: Solving Design Challenges with Young Children*. Washington, DC: NAEYC.

Howard, T.C. 2019. "Capitalizing on Culture: Engaging Young Learners in Diverse Classrooms." In *Spotlight on Young Children: Equity and Diversity*, eds. C. Gillanders & R. Procopio, 31–44. Washington, DC: NAEYC.

Huffman, J.M., & C. Fortenberry. 2011. "Helping Preschoolers Prepare for Writing: Developing Fine Motor Skills." *Young Children* 66 (5): 100–3.

Hynes-Berry, M., & L. Grandau. 2019. *Where's the Math? Books, Games, and Routines to Spark Children's Thinking*. Washington, DC: NAEYC.

Isenberg, J.P., & M.R. Jalongo. 2018. *Creative Thinking and Arts-Based Learning: Preschool Through Fourth Grade*. 7th ed. New York: Pearson.

Johnston, D.W., M.E.R. Nicholls, M. Shah, & M.A. Shields. 2009. "Nature's Experiment? Handedness and Early Childhood Development." *Demography* 46 (2): 281–301.

Jones, J. 2018. "Reframing the Assessment Discussion." In *Spotlight on Young Children: Observation and Assessment*, eds. H. Bohart & R. Procopio, 6–14. Washington, DC: NAEYC.

Joseph, G.E., & P.S. Strain. 2003. "Enhancing Emotional Vocabulary in Young Children." *Young Exceptional Children* 6 (4): 18–26.

Józsa, K., & K.C. Barrett. 2018. "Affective and Social Mastery Motivation in Preschool as Predictors of Early School Success: A Longitudinal Study." *Early Childhood Research Quarterly* 45 (4): 81–92.

Kahn, P.H., Jr., T. Weiss, & K. Harrington. 2018. "Modeling Child–Nature Interaction in a Nature Preschool: A Proof of Concept." *Frontiers in Psychology* 9: 835. doi:10.3389 /fpsyg.2018.00835.

Kamdar, K. 2020. "Connecting Culture and Play: Practical Strategies for Educators." In *Each and Every Child: Teaching Preschool with an Equity Lens*, eds. S. Friedman & A. Mwenelupembe, 29–32. Washington, DC: NAEYC.

Levin, D.E. 2013. *Beyond Remote-Controlled Childhood: Teaching Young Children in the Media Age*. Washington, DC: NAEYC.

Lin, L.-Y., R.-J. Cherng, & Y.-J. Chen. 2017. "Effect of Touch Screen Tablet Use on Fine Motor Development of Young Children." *Physical and Occupational Therapy in Pediatrics* 37 (5): 457–67.

Logue, M.E., & A. Detour. 2011. "'You Be the Bad Guy': A New Role for Teachers in Supporting Children's Dramatic Play." *Early Childhood Research and Practice* 13 (1). https://ecrp.illinois.edu/v13n1/logue.html.

MA DESE (Massachusetts Department of Elementary and Secondary Education). 2016. "2016 Massachusetts Science and Technology/Engineering (STE) Curriculum Framework." Malden, MA: MA DESE. www.doe.mass.edu/frameworks/scitech /2016-04.pdf.

McMullen, M.B., & D. Brody. 2022. *Infants and Toddlers at Play: Choosing the Right Stuff for Learning and Development*. Washington, DC: NAEYC.

Meier, D., & S. Sisk-Hilton. 2017 "Nature and Environmental Education in Early Childhood." *The New Educator* 13 (3): 191–94.

Mooney, C.G. 2013. *Theories of Childhood: An Introduction to Dewey, Montessori, Erikson, Piaget, and Vygotsky*. 2nd ed. St. Paul, MN: Redleaf Press.

Mooney, C.G. 2018. *Choose Your Words: Communicating with Young Children*. 2nd ed. St. Paul, MN: Redleaf Press.

Moreno, R., & R. Mayer. 2007. "Interactive Multimodal Learning Environments." *Educational Psychology Review* 19 (3): 309–26.

NAEYC. 2019. "Advancing Equity in Early Childhood Education." Position statement. Washington, DC: NAEYC. www.naeyc.org/resources/position-statements/equity.

NAEYC. 2020. "Developmentally Appropriate Practice." Position statement. Washington, DC: NAEYC. www.naeyc.org/resources/position-statements/dap.

NAEYC. 2022. *Developmentally Appropriate Practice in Early Childhood Programs Serving Children from Birth Through Age 8*. 4th ed. Washington, DC: NAEYC.

New Jersey Department of Education. 2014. *Preschool Teaching and Learning Standards*. Trenton, NJ: New Jersey Department of Education. www.nj.gov/education/ece/guide /standards.pdf.

New Jersey Department of Education. 2015. *Preschool Program Implementation Guidelines*. Trenton, NJ: New Jersey Department of Education. www.nj.gov/education /ece/guide/impguidelines.pdf.

NYS ED (New York State Education Department). 2019. "Resource Guides for School Success: The Prekindergarten Early Learning Standards." Albany, NY: NYS ED. http://nysed.gov/common/nysed/files/programs/early-learning/pk-standards -resource-web-revised-2021.pdf.

Ozmun, J.C., & D.L. Gallahue. 2017. "Motor Development." In *Adapted Physical Education and Sport*, 6th ed., eds. J.P. Winnick & D.L. Porretta, 375–90. Champaign, IL: Human Kinetics.

Partnership for 21st Century Learning. 2019. *21st Century Learning for Early Childhood Framework*. Hilliard, OH: Battelle for Kids. http://static.battelleforkids.org/documents /p21/P21EarlyChildhoodFramework.pdf.

Pilonieta, P., P.L. Shue, & B.T. Kissel. 2019. "Reading Books, Writing Books: Reading and Writing Come Together in a Dual Language Classroom." In *Spotlight on Young Children: Equity and Diversity*, eds. C. Gillanders & R. Procopio, 75–84. Washington, DC: NAEYC.

Ramanathan, G., D. Carter, & J. Wenner. 2021. "A Framework for Scientific Inquiry in Preschool." *Early Childhood Education Journal*. doi:10.1007/s10643-021-01259-1.

Rideout, V., & M.B. Robb. 2020. *The Common Sense Census: Media Use by Kids Age Zero to Eight*. Report. San Francisco: Common Sense Media. www.commonsensemedia.org /sites/default/files/uploads/research/2020_zero_to_eight_census_final_web.pdf.

Rumenapp, J.C., P.Z. Morales, & A.M. Lykouretzos. 2018. "Building a Cohesive Multimodal Environment for Diverse Learners." *Young Children* 73 (5): 72–78.

Schaal, B., T.K. Saxton, H. Loos, R. Soussignan, & K. Durand. 2020. "Olfaction Scaffolds the Developing Human from Neonate to Adolescent and Beyond." *Philosophical Transactions of the Royal Society B* 375 (1800): e1–e15.

Shuster, C. 2000. "Emotions Count: Scaffolding Children's Representations of Themselves and Their Feelings to Develop Emotional Intelligence." Paper presented at Issues in Early Childhood Education: Curriculum, Teacher Education, and Dissemination of Information, Lilian Katz Symposium, in Champaign, IL.

Souto, P.H.S., J.N. Santos, H.R. Leite, M. Hadders-Algra, S.C. Guedes, J.N.P. Nobre, L.R. Santos, & R.L. de Souza Morais. 2020. "Tablet Use in Young Children Is Associated with Advanced Fine Motor Skills." *Journal of Motor Behavior* 52 (2): 196–203.

Stodden, D.F., J.D. Goodway, S.J. Langendorfer, M.A. Roberton, M.E. Rudisill, C. Garcia, & L.E. Garcia. 2012. "A Developmental Perspective on the Role of Motor Skill Competence in Physical Activity: An Emergent Relationship." *Quest* 60 (2): 290–306.

Strasser, J., & L.M. Bresson. 2017. *Big Questions for Young Minds: Extending Children's Thinking*. Washington, DC: NAEYC.

Tapia, K., E. Pickering, & J.R. Coffino. 2021. "Stepping Back to Nurture." *Teaching Young Children* 15 (1): 18–20.

Tominey, S.L., E.C. O'Bryon, S.E. Rivers, & S. Shapses. 2017. "Teaching Emotional Intelligence in Early Childhood." *Young Children* 72 (1): 6–12.

Torres, M.M., C.E. Domitrovich, & K.L. Bierman. 2015. "Preschool Interpersonal Relationships Predict Kindergarten Achievement: Mediated by Gains in Emotional Knowledge." *Journal of Applied Developmental Psychology* 39: 44–52.

Trelease, J., & C. Giorgis. 2019. *Jim Trelease's Read-Aloud Handbook*. 8th ed. New York: Penguin Books.

Turrou, A.C., N.C. Johnson, & M.L. Franke. 2021. *The Young Child and Mathematics*. 3rd ed. Washington, DC: NAEYC.

University of Leeds. 2018. "Children with Better Coordination More Likely to Achieve at School." *ScienceDaily*, July 11. www.sciencedaily.com/releases/2018/07/180711093224.htm.

Waldron, N. 2020. "Will You Pass the Peas, Please?" *Teaching Young Children* 13 (4): 22–23.

Wanless, S.B., & P.A. Crawford. With S. Friedman. 2020. "Books That Support Diversity, Conversations, and Play." In *Each and Every Child: Teaching Preschool with an Equity Lens*, eds. S. Friedman & A. Mwenelupembe, 60–63. Washington, DC: NAEYC.

Wasik, B.A., & A.H. Hindman. 2018. "Why Wait? The Importance of Wait Time in Developing Young Students' Language and Vocabulary Skills." *The Reading Teacher* 72 (3): 369–78.

Wexler, N. 2020. "A Stronger Foundation: Connecting Teaching to the Science of Learning." Viewpoint. *Young Children* 75 (2): 80–84.

Whitney, T. 2002. *Kids Like Us: Using Persona Dolls in the Classroom*. St. Paul, MN: Redleaf Press.

Yogman, M., A. Garner, J. Hutchinson, K. Hirsh-Pasek, & R.M. Golinkoff. 2018. "The Power of Play: A Pediatric Role in Enhancing Development." Clinical Report. Pediatrics 142 (3): 1–18.

Resources

Articles

Bresson, L.M., M. King, L. Brahms, & P.S. Wardrip. 2017. "Create Problems for Your Preschoolers, Don't Solve Them! *Making* in Your Learning Centers." *Teaching Young Children* 10 (4): 12–15.

Cutler, C. n.d. "Support Math with Materials in Your Home." *NAEYC for Families.* www.naeyc.org/our-work/families/support-math-materials-your-home.

Schaefer, R. 2016. "Teacher Inquiry on the Influence of Materials on Children's Learning." Voices of Practitioners. *Young Children* 71 (5): 64–73.

Books

Alanís, I., M.G. Arreguín, & I. Salinas-González. 2021. *The Essentials: Supporting Dual Language Learners in Diverse Environments in Preschool and Kindergarten.* Washington, DC: NAEYC.

Brillante, P. 2017. *The Essentials: Supporting Young Children with Disabilities in the Classroom.* Washington, DC: NAEYC.

Carlson, F.M. 2011. *Big Body Play: Why Boisterous, Vigorous, and Very Physical Play Is Essential to Children's Development and Learning.* Washington, DC: NAEYC.

Choosy Kids. 2018. *Move and Learn with Choosy.* Charlotte, NC: Choosy Kids.

Daly, L., & M. Beloglovsky. 2015. *Loose Parts: Inspiring Play in Young Children.* St. Paul, MN: Redleaf Press.

Dombro, A.L., J. Jablon, & C. Stetson. 2020. *Powerful Interactions: How to Connect with Children to Extend Their Learning.* 2nd ed. Washington, DC: NAEYC.

Editors of *Teaching Young Children.* 2015. *Exploring Math and Science in Preschool.* Washington, DC: NAEYC.

Editors of *Teaching Young Children.* 2015. *Expressing Creativity in Preschool.* Washington, DC: NAEYC.

Editors of *Teaching Young Children.* 2015. *Learning About Language and Literacy in Preschool.* Washington, DC: NAEYC.

Elkind, D. 2007. *The Power of Play: Learning What Comes Naturally.* Boston: Da Capo Press.

Friedman, S., & A. Mwenelupembe, eds. 2020. *Each and Every Child: Teaching Preschool with an Equity Lens.* Washington, DC: NAEYC.

Hanscom, A.J. 2016. *Balanced and Barefoot: How Unrestricted Outdoor Play Makes for Strong, Confident, and Capable Children.* Oakland, CA: New Harbinger Publications.

Harms, T., R.M. Clifford, & D. Cryer. 2014. *Early Childhood Environment Rating Scale.* 3rd ed. New York: Teachers College Press.

Heroman, C. 2017. *Making and Tinkering with STEM: Solving Design Challenges with Young Children.* Washington, DC: NAEYC.

Hynes-Berry, M., & L. Grandau. 2019. *Where's the Math? Books, Games, and Routines to Spark Children's Thinking.* Washington, DC: NAEYC.

Isbell, R., & S.A. Yoshizawa. 2016. *Nurturing Creativity: An Essential Mindset for Young Children's Learning.* Washington, DC: NAEYC.

Jones, E., & G. Reynolds. 2011. *The Play's the Thing: Teachers' Roles in Children's Play.* 2nd ed. New York: Teachers College Press.

Lambert, M.D. 2015. *Reading Picture Books with Children: How to Shake Up Storytime and Get Kids Talking About What They See.* Watertown, MA: Charlesbridge.

Masterson, M.L., & H. Bohart, eds. 2019. *Serious Fun: How Guided Play Extends Children's Learning.* Washington, DC: NAEYC.

Mraz, K., A. Porcelli, & C. Tyler. 2016. *Purposeful Play: A Teacher's Guide to Igniting Deep and Joyful Learning Across the Day.* Portsmouth, NH: Heinemann.

Murphy, L. 2016. *Lisa Murphy on Play: The Foundation of Children's Learning.* 2nd ed. St. Paul, MN: Redleaf Press.

Nell, M.L., & W.F. Drew. With D.E. Bush. 2013. *From Play to Practice: Connecting Teachers' Play to Children's Learning.* Washington, DC: NAEYC.

Pecaski McLennan, D. 2020. *Embracing Math: Cultivating a Mindset for Exploring and Learning.* Washington, DC: NAEYC.

Schickedanz, J.A., & M.F. Collins. 2012. *So Much More than the ABCs: The Early Phases of Reading and Writing.* Washington, DC: NAEYC.

Strasser, J., & L.M. Bresson. 2017. *Big Questions for Young Minds: Extending Children's Thinking.* Washington, DC: NAEYC.

Turrou, A.C., N.C. Johnson, & M.L. Franke. 2021. *The Young Child and Mathematics.* 3rd ed. Washington, DC: NAEYC.

Online

- **Center on the Social and Emotional Foundations for Early Learning (CSEFEL):** http://csefel.vanderbilt.edu
- **The Children's Book Review:** www.thechildrensbookreview.com
- **Common Sense Media:** www.commonsensemedia.org
- **The Freecycle Network:** www.freecycle.org
- **Games for Young Mathematicians:** http://youngmathematicians.edc.org
- **National Association for the Exchange of Industrial Resources (NAEIR):** www.naeir.org
- **The Preschool Athlete:** https://preschoolathlete.com
- **Reusable Resources Association (RRA):** www.reuseresources.org

Index

Page numbers followed by *f* and *t* indicate figures and tables, respectively.

Acknowledgments

The authors would like to thank several people who made significant contributions to this book as resources and thought partners: our editors, Rossella Procopio and Susan Friedman, who always provided thoughtful and intuitive feedback; Dr. Holly Seplocha, whose love of children's books is evidenced in the titles she shared to enhance each chapter; and Kathy Charner, who planted the seed for this project and watched from afar while it blossomed.

Lisa is incredibly grateful to her husband, Jason, and children, Levi and Jacob, for their infinite patience during the writing process. In the words of her husband, "Living with Lisa is like living in one of those high pressure HGTV shows! You never know what you're gonna get!" Also, to the individuals who have always believed in *everything* she does: her mother, Jeannie Singletary; her late father and "bonus mom," Jay and Annette Mufson; and her "bonus dads" Bruce Singletary and Robert Strasser. Your devotion is forever motivating. She also honors her mentor and friend Janis Strasser for being the best reflective thought partner any author could ask for. Lisa treasures the support of these folks more than words could ever describe.

To Lisa's former colleagues at Grow NJ Kids, thanks for being available to listen and reflect about her "next big idea" throughout the writing process, from start to finish!

And last, but definitely not least, Lisa holds deep gratitude for her soul-deep friendships, her chosen family, who pushed beyond, deconstructed questions, and held space so she could find the answers she needed while crafting this text. Magical, unique, and simply wonder-full, you are truly the bee's knees!

Megan would like to thank her family for their enduring support and encouragement; her partner, Jeffrey, for his patience, confidence, and commitment; her sister, Kellianne, for providing a laugh when it was gravely needed; her mother, Frances, for sharing her passion for education and instilling a deep sense of responsibility to the children we teach; and her late father, Andrew, who believed in and unwaveringly supported everything she does.

Megan would also like to thank her colleagues and friends in Passaic Public Schools who inspire her with their ideas and excitement for teaching young children, especially Ketty Perez, Megan's teaching partner for the past seven years who never questions the materials she brings into the classroom; Dana Pergola, who is always willing to jump out on the ledge with Megan and try something new; and Marilin Machado, who many years ago shared her passion for teaching young children and opened a door in Megan's life.

Lastly, Megan would like to thank the children and families with whom she has been privileged to work. They have inspired her in countless ways with their excitement, involvement, and commitment.

We have deep appreciation for the many children in our lives. We acknowledge the golden threads that connect us to the children of our past, our present, and even our futures. We celebrate the children we work with and our love for teaching and learning. During one of our conversations in which Megan was remembering how much she enjoyed being with her preschoolers after a particularly difficult day, she paused for a moment and said matter-of-factly, "They're my best friends."

About the Authors

Lisa Mufson Bresson, MEd, is an early childhood education consultant with Beyond Boundaries, LLC, and coauthor of NAEYC's bestselling book *Big Questions for Young Minds: Extending Children's Thinking*. She leads workshops and presentations at local, state, national, and international conferences, thriving on the connections she makes with learners—both big and little!—on a daily basis. Since 2008, she has been a contributing author to *Teaching Young Children (TYC)*, NAEYC's magazine for preschool teachers, and serves on *TYC*'s advisory board. She is a former program manager for Grow NJ Kids, New Jersey's statewide Quality Rating and Improvement System for early childhood programs. Previously, Lisa taught in urban public preschool settings for over a decade.

Megan King, MEd, is a preschool teacher at Passaic Public Schools in Passaic, New Jersey. She has worked in the field of early childhood education for over 15 years. She is active in the makerspace movement and has presented on and coauthored several articles about incorporating hands-on "maker" materials in early childhood classrooms. She has written articles published in *TYC* and is proud to serve as one of *TYC*'s advisory board members. She worked with a diverse group of early childhood educators on the NAEYC/PBS Ready To Learn Content Review Advisory Board and is a past NJ Governor's Educator of the Year Award winner at the school level. Megan enjoys working with her preschoolers and experiencing the world through their eyes.